FAULKNER

A HOCKEY HISTORY

TOM ROSSITER

BREAKWATER

100 Water Street, St. John's, NL, Canada, A1C 6E6
WWW.BREAKWATERBOOKS.COM

A CIP catalogue record for this book is available from Library and Archives Canada.
ISBN 978-1-55081-376-0
Copyright © 2011 Tom Rossiter

Canada Council   Conseil des Arts   Canadä   Newfoundland
for the Arts   du Canada   Labrador

We acknowledge the support of the Canada Council for the Arts which last year invested $20.1 million in writing and publishing throughout Canada. We acknowledge the Government of Canada through the Canada Book Fund and the Government of Newfoundland and Labrador through the Department of Tourism, Culture and Recreation for our publishing activities.

PRINTED AND BOUND IN CANADA.

FIRST, THERE WAS THE LOVE OF THE GAME...

Everybody wanted to play hockey. It was the one thing you could do
in the wintertime ... you'd go on a river, or on a pond that'd freeze
over somewhere ... and you'd make an old wooden scraper somehow,
and you'd scrape off the snow, and you'd play ... wherever you could
get a bit of ice to skate on, you'd play.

... THEN THE DREAM OF BECOMING A PRO.

There were only six NHL teams back then, so you're talking
120 players ... and the rest of the guys had to play in the minor
leagues if they wanted to play hockey, and wait and hope that
someone might get hurt or something, and you'd get a call-up.
That's what you had ahead of you.

PART FOUR

WORLD ICE HOCKEY CHAMPIONSHIPS: TEAM CANADA, 1966

PART FIVE

THE SEMI-FINALS: 1967-1971

PART SIX

THE FINALS: 1975-1979

FOREWORD

IN A CAREER THAT SPANNED four decades, George Faulkner became Newfoundland's premier athlete, and, in the opinion of many, its best hockey player.

His story, in many respects, is the story of the Faulkner family itself. The five hockey-playing brothers, three of whom would go on to play professionally, were nurtured by Lester Faulkner, a father reminiscent, in his dedication to his sons and to the game itself, of Walter Gretzky and the commitment he made to his famous son, Wayne, probably the best player in the game ever.

Most people remember George Faulkner as being a victim of circumstance in his effort to make the NHL: the timing of his young professional career with the Montreal organization coming when the Canadiens dominated the hockey world and the Stanley Cup for almost a decade. But the story is not that simple. There were other circumstances in his career that would take him close, but, each time, not quite there.

A few years ago, younger brother Alex, who went on to play with the Toronto Maple Leafs and the Detroit Red Wings, attended an old-timers' reunion, and remembers a conversation he had with Montreal's two-time scoring champ, Dickie Moore. Moore remembered George Faulkner quite well. His comment to Alex: "George Faulkner was the best player I ever saw who never played in the NHL."

This is the story of how all that happened, and more.

PART ONE

THE JUNIOR YEARS

1951-1954

1

BEGINNINGS

His first skating experience was by way of tin cans crushed onto winter boots, and a long, long slide across a patch of frozen street water.

Kids everywhere stomped young legs into milk or soup cans until the cans buckled enough to fit, then skated ('slid') crazily back and forth to the end of small strips of ice, wherever they could find them. A lot of fun, but far from the real thing.

In a way though, thinking back to those days, it really was like the real thing because it was all in the balance you showed in skating, no matter what you wore. Even at so early an age, he was showing he understood the far-reaching importance of this facet of the game, an understanding well beyond his years.

IN SWEDEN, THE WORD IS 'TIMMERHUGGARE.'

The terms "lumberjack" and "woodcutter" have largely faded from use in modern times, losing their romantic aura years ago to worldwide advances in technology in the industry. The manpower needed to produce pulp and paper for the world's huge paper mills has become the work of a machine-driven work force, relegating the role of the lumberjack to largely a thing of the past. Sweden itself fell victim to technology at about the time of the Industrial Revolution. Its lumber industry, the so-called first industry of many European countries, was the largest in Europe, its forests covering nearly 70 percent of the country's entire land mass.

It was the opening up of this world of lumber, pulp and paper, and paper mills that brought the descendants of the Faulkner family to Newfoundland. No one remembers the exact date of their arrival but it would surely have coincided with the development of the giant paper mill at Grand Falls (1909) and its subsidiary work forces in the logging and pulp-making industries at Bishop's Falls. Plans for the mill began a few years before when the A.N.D. (Anglo-Newfoundland Development) Company was formed, its launching attracting workers from all over Newfoundland, Canada, the United States and Europe. The town of Grand Falls would remain a company town until 1961 when A.N.D. forfeited its rights to Abitibi-Price Inc. and the first municipal elections were held in the new town.

However, it is unclear why the Lindahl family, living in northern Sweden at the turn of the twentieth century, would have immigrated to Newfoundland at a time when most of their countrymen were settling in Minnesota. A large Swedish community was already being established there, with abundant rich farmland available and a prosperous lumber industry to draw on. We can assume their situation was no different from that of many European families of that era: scarcity of work, better wages abroad, including the prospect of land ownership, and, in some cases, freedom from a state-dominated religious system which showed itself to be anything but tolerant of those wanting to practice outside the norm.

Newfoundland, with its British history and well-known attachments to the old country, probably seemed the ideal place to guarantee the newcomer and his family both security and permanence. As well, the new mill could offer a promising future in a country whose landscape and lifestyle were strikingly similar to the homeland they had just left. In particular, lumberjacks, men whose back-breaking job was still in demand to supply the raw material for the mill, like the *timmerhuggare* of Sweden, were more than welcome.

The family disembarked from their long journey at Lewisporte in 1907, and from there eventually made their way to Bishop's Falls, nearer the heart of the lumber industry and the huge mill under construction at the time. 'Grandpa and Grandma' Lindahl was all anyone in the family ever remembers calling them, their first names being somehow lost to history. They brought with them a family of six children: three boys and three girls, the oldest of whom was a very beautiful daughter, Svea, about 14 years old. Svea was to become grandmother to the Faulkner lineage and probably the first of the Lindahl family to be remembered by a first name.

The beautiful Svea Lindahl married William Faulkner from Sherbrooke, Nova Scotia, who, like so many others in those years, had heard of the good work prospects in Grand Falls and had moved to Newfoundland looking for a new life in its vibrant lumber industry. William and Svea had eleven children, including George's father, Lester, who was to become, like all the others, a woodsman contracted to supply pulpwood to the Bishop's Falls operation.

The promise of winter in Newfoundland's central region is always fulfilled. Snowfall is a constant, winter temperatures often holding the land in sub-Arctic fashion – idyllic, in its way, for the game of hockey.

The Exploits River, the largest and perhaps coldest in Newfoundland, is a frozen spectre at all its points as it moves past the town to the falls, and then to the sea. The line of winter is only broken here and there along its banks where a community hockey rink has been shaped out of its ruggedness. Its use is in every way a community affair: older folk coming out before daylight to groom and refurbish after a day, like every other, full of games and skating.

The Faulkner family's early association with railway folk allowed them a special and rather privileged spot on the river, a place called Roundhouse Cove. As the name suggests, the rink was fashioned near the railway's roundhouse operation, a convenient location next to their workplace, where a specialized group of men called "hustlers" tended the rink faithfully every winter. Hustlers prepared the trains for their journeys inland: filling water tanks, greasing drivers and loading the coal tenders – a considerable work grind in the old railway system of years ago. Nevertheless, it was understood that part of their assignment each night during the winter season was to keep the rink in the cove operational as well, no matter what. All that was missing of any real importance in their hockey world was any amount of player equipment, especially all-important jocks and shin pads. The need for such vital equipment created a long-standing rule during the games that they were not allowed to "rise" the puck under any circumstances. If they did, through some over-eager display or another, and someone lay injured – all hell would break loose.

Competition between communities in other areas in central Newfoundland was already well underway with the opening of the Grand Falls Arena, just a few miles away. Not to be outdone, the people of Bishop's Falls soon organized an outdoor rink of their own, not far from Roundhouse Cove itself. Prefabricated boards soon lined the surface area, together with outdoor lighting, dressing rooms and even toilet facilities. Each game was a fully organized affair, with referees, fully dressed goalies, 11-12 players per team and some version or other of makeshift team uniforms. The reason for such generous arrangements lay in the town's dual social structure in which the plant, a newcomer on the block made up of pulp mill workers, representing and living in one section of town, worked together with the more established "station" people, representing the railway system, in another. Together they formed an amiable social network that operated in a comfortable, easygoing way all year. Now, for the first time, the small community could invite real competition from outside on a regular basis with teams from Grand Falls, Badger, Botwood and Buchans becoming frequent visitors.

The dominance that had prevailed initially by the bigger and more experienced players in the small town soon wilted in the face of a surge of young players, including three young Faulkner boys – Lindy, George and Alex – who would go on to dominate the game not just against the plant, but much of the larger central area as well.

Second only to the rink at Roundhouse Cove, the Faulkner household was quickly becoming its own hockey shrine, led by the interest of the father, Lester, who became manager, coach and mentor of the three older boys. At Christmas time he saw that each one stepped on the ice fitted out in new hockey regalia, recently arrived by train from the T. Eaton Company in Halifax. The boys called the train, the way train, since they knew it had "come from away" with all their seasonal and Christmas stuff packaged on board, and they knew full well the contents of each package as it was being unloaded – mostly hockey equipment.

Lester Faulkner never played organized hockey as a kid but, according to George, he had the skills to be a good one. Soccer was his game growing up more so than hockey, and it was the biggest summer sport in the area for many years, but especially in the 1940s. He made sure the boys played as well. Each year he'd see his way to make a buying trip to St. John's and as a matter of course would return with several pairs of soccer boots for the boys – often second-hand and mismatching pairs. Appearances mattered little back then.

But it was hockey that he concentrated on most with his boys. He'd often go into the woods before the hockey season began to cut pieces of birchwood he'd find shaped like hockey sticks, later using an axe to flatten them as near as possible into the required shape. What turned out was often a cross between the round blade of a field hockey stick and the flat, rectangular shape of the real thing. George remembers also, when the river was frozen and hockey well underway in the town, how his father joined the hustlers, cleaning and flooding the ice each night to make ready for the next day's action.

Another custom in the Faulkner home during the hockey season was for Lester to call the boys in the pre-dawn darkness – dark, freezing mornings – have them out of bed, breakfast served and on their way to the river for an hour's skating before they left for school. More often than not, when the skating session finished, they'd simply continue skating on down the river to the schoolhouse nearby for the day's "academic" exercise, their hearts and minds almost certainly still back on the river.

On Saturdays, however, before anyone left the house to play hockey, he would make sure that each of the boys had completed the day's chores.

> We couldn't wait for Saturdays to come, to get a day off from school. We had chores to do first: saw up wood first of all, because we weren't allowed to saw wood on Sundays, or bring in the wood on Sundays or bring water. We had a barrel in our porch, we'd fill that up with water from the well because there was no running water in the house, and then cut up enough wood, birch or spruce or whatever was there, and make sure the woodbox was full before we were allowed to go over to the river to play hockey.

Sunday was devoted to church and family in the Faulkner home:

> We weren't allowed to play on Sundays. We'd have to go to church three times that day, and Mom would stay home and do the cooking. Most of the times she's have a roast in the oven, probably a roast of moose. Most families lived on moose in those times.

It seems likely that every household in the community was doing the same thing on Saturdays in Bishop's Falls back then, to be followed by a great rush of children – almost en masse – to the Exploits River to begin the day's fun. And it would be long after dark before they headed home, leaving a deserted landscape to be swept clean and flooded again later that night for the next day.

On one particular Saturday, a friend of the family, Ray Temple, came to the Faulkners' house and asked George if he could borrow his skates for a make-up game later that day. The skates were in such bad shape that when Temple returned them, he suggested they meet over at Whiteway's Store on Monday coming. "We went to have a look around, to see what they had in skates. There was this nice-looking pair, with a strap and buckle support across the arch. The blades had to be riveted on. Ray paid thirteen dollars for them – my first pair of new skates." George was 14 at the time.

The day would finish for the boys when they'd tune in to the weekly hockey broadcasts on the family kitchen radio. The Faulkner brothers, like every other kid in Newfoundland and Canada back then, followed Foster Hewitt's *Hockey Night in Canada* every Saturday night from Toronto. They couldn't wait for the broadcast each week, although they never knew from one week to the next if the old radio would hold up long enough for just one more game. There was always the thought that the relic would finally sputter out and die, or just go on giving them more trouble, a routine nuisance every week. The radio was an old-timer, a small brown Emerson, and it always acted up during the broadcast, almost as if some mischievous spirit were inside – something that didn't like hockey. The sound was sure to fade and come back, fade and come back, upsetting the whole kitchen assembly. George explained how they managed to keep it going until the end of the game:

> We used to pinch the wire at the back of the radio. The forefinger and thumb would be right sore after the game, trying to get it to come in better. Trying to get the ground working. As soon as we'd hear Foster die out we'd pinch the wire at the back of the radio – it's a wonder we never got a shock or got killed.

There are no family pictures of the Faulkner children preparing for their first day of school, nor of any of the boys waving a cheerful goodbye from the end of the garden path. At least not one of young George. He admits he was no lover of the academic life.

School was another world away for him, fairly well removed from his only real love at the time, as he readily admits: "I never did like school. I couldn't get out fast enough. But our parents kept after us, never let up on emphasizing the importance of education, so I had no choice but to continue. And glad that I did. As a matter of fact, in my last year of school, dad wanted me to be a dentist, but I was so glad to get out of school, it wasn't even funny. I never told my boys any of that. They'll learn about that when they read it in the book."

The place of schooling in the lives of the Faulkner children was in fact a practical matter, with opportunities for permanent work available either at the mill or with the railway the moment they finished school. At age 16, George found himself as a "student fireman" with the railway, servicing a steam engine on its runs west to Grand Falls. He worked only one trip on his own, "getting the boiler up just below two hundred pounds of steam, injecting the water in her, with a little dart of oil once in a while." It might have been a full-time career, had it not been for his love of hockey.

His experience in the working world of the Newfoundland railway would be short-lived. In the next year, 1951, at age 17, he would quit his job and leave home for a hockey tryout in Quebec City. He'd find himself repeating the same pattern the following year – beginning permanent work on his return home during the summer, this time at the paper mill in Grand Falls, and then quitting once more, moving on again in an attempt this time to make the jump to the Junior "A" level. At age 18, he would already have left two permanent positions at home to try his future in hockey, each time speculating on where it might take him.

Little did he realize at the time it would become a lifelong quest.

2

HOME AND AWAY

THE OLD GAME WAS BORN IN THE NORTH.

It emerged from the far, snow-filled reaches of Canada, from the frozen wilderness of its lakes and rivers, the remote small towns of the Prairies, the vast stretches of Ontario's hinterland, and the wintry mosaic of a thousand and one villages in Quebec.

Back in the 1940s and 1950s, young hopefuls were drawn from anonymity in these secluded settings across the north and invited to play the game at a level they never thought possible. It would be a journey that would transform many of them into legends of the sport across the country.

Kids like Howe, Balfour, Bentley, Bathgate, Eziniki, Mosienko, Sawchuk, Olmstead, Bucyk, Gadsby, Barilko, Hillman, Backstrom and Mahovlich were uprooted from friends and family and invited to travel east, to the big cities of Montreal and Toronto, or perhaps even farther from home to cities in the United States they'd probably never even heard of. The intimate surroundings of hometowns where, almost from the time they had learned to walk, they had gathered every year to play the game, would be forever behind them.

Train and bus rides into the unknown opened up to them, bringing their game to an unfamiliar world of first-time training camps; coaches they looked up to in awe; real playing equipment in personalized locker room stalls; and, not least, their first playing experience in a brightly lit indoor arena. Here, for the first time, many were to play the game in a confined space and were pressed quickly to adjust to the first of many difficult techniques of this game – playing the puck off the boards, judging its angles for passing and clearing as it caromed and deflected in every possible direction.

"Scrimmages" in this new world would soon take on a different dimension from the helter-skelter playmaking on the rivers and backyard rinks they had just left. They would have to endure skating, passing and shooting drills to no end, learn defensive maneuvers ("what you do when you don't have the puck") and told – emphatically – to "head-man the puck" at all times, a move that, unless it was performed without fail every time, would drive coaches into a frenzy. Defencemen, in particular, were trained and specialized in a host of their own more aggressive moves, especially the all-important "one-on-one" and "two-on-one" drills. They practiced these ad nauseam, and whenever they failed in this drill they were reminded each time – by way of a coach's bellowing heard round the rink – to "get the *#@&* man, not the *#@&* puck."

And on and on it went.

But always, first and foremost, as they had surely been told from day one back home, it was their skating abilities that mattered most, a fundamental of the game like no other. It would immediately separate the strong from the weak, the skilled from the less experienced. A myriad of drills enforced the point: forwards, backwards, sideways, figure eights, stops and starts, jumping the circles – every imaginable pattern, every contortion the human frame could endure. They soon realized that despite their youthful strength and enthusiasm at this stage of their lives, the skating drills would bring them to their knees every time, literally.

The town of Grand Falls opened its new stadium in 1947, and that same year introduced Gordie Drillon to the central Newfoundland area. Drillon had played seven years in the NHL, six with Toronto and one with Montreal, before quitting back in 1943 to join the war effort. He'd won the Art Ross and Lady Byng trophies with Toronto, and despite having only a very brief career with the pros, his scoring records earned him a place in the Hockey Hall of Fame in 1975.

His style of play was to put a different focus on the game. Drillon concentrated much of his goal-scoring ability in the "slot," putting extra pressure on the goalie and the defence, who now had a double-duty – trying to keep abreast of the play elsewhere inside their blueline, while struggling to manhandle someone like Drillon directly in front of the net. Decades later, players like Phil Esposito and Dino Ciccarelli imitated this style of play to great success, especially during the more critical phase of the season – the playoffs. More than just being effective in the slot, Drillon, who stood six feet and weighed 186 pounds, was a natural goal scorer with a deadly accurate shot, as remembered by the Toronto

Maple Leaf goalie of that era, Turk Broda: "I don't think there's a player in hockey who can shoot the puck more accurately. Even if you leave him an opening the size of the puck, he'll hit it every time."

Drillon, born in Moncton, New Brunswick, was hired on by the Leafs in 1947 as a hockey scout for teams in the Maritimes. It seems one of his early assignments might have been to Grand Falls and, as luck would have it, to take a first look at prospects in the area, especially young George Faulkner.

Faulkner had just turned 16 around the time of Drillon's arrival. The meeting of the two coincided nicely with a visit of the NHL's New York Rangers shortly after the opening of the stadium. The Rangers had missed the playoffs that year, finishing in last place, and had immediately put together an exhibition tour of the Maritimes. As happened every spring in hockey, the two teams missing the playoffs each year would go on tour – one to western Canada, the other to the east. The extra money to be made on such trips went a long way to prop up their meager salaries at the time. It was also a good way to close out the season and enjoy the game from a totally different perspective.*

Gordie Drillon decided to add some flavour to the exhibition match by having a 16-year-old upstart dress for the game and join the Grand Falls lineup. Young Faulkner had a surprise in store for veteran Ranger goalie Chuck Rayner, known for coming out of his net to challenge oncoming players. In this case, the young Faulkner beat him to the puck, went around him and scored into an empty net. The stadium erupted. To this day, George wondered about that goal: "I think Rayner just let me score."

George had already met Drillon briefly during practice earlier with nine or ten others from the Bishop's Falls high school team. He remembered his first encounter with the big and imposing ex-NHL star:

> I remember it was early in the morning – six o'clock in the morning and I was playing centre ice. I remember him dropping the puck, and I just took it and went on in and scored a goal. I came back and we centred off and I took the puck again and scored another goal. He came over to me then and tapped me on the

---

* The 1955-56 Boston Bruins finished fifth that year and toured the Maritimes, playing one game at the newly opened St. John's Memorial Stadium.

shoulder, 'You better go in now and sit down in the box and watch the other guys play.' I kind of figured what he was up to.

Skating was the big difference in Faulkner's play, even then. He could easily outskate the rest. As he recalled, when he'd hit the other team's blueline, "There'd be no one there so I'd skate in alone and just score."

His play was compelling throughout his high school years. His success and popularity at this level continued to grow, and would take an interesting twist during a Christmas home visit two years later with another chance to get back at an old high school rival – Grand Falls Academy. In the meantime the dominance would continue, his play largely unchallenged by kids his own age. In truth, he could stay competitive beyond the high school level, playing brief shifts in both junior and senior league play. Little did he realize at the time that in just two years he would progress from a 12-game regular-season schedule at home, to a 60-game schedule in Quebec, and the one-dimensional patterns of the game he was so familiar with would be a thing of the past.

That was how it started for George Faulkner. A coach and outstanding player from the professional ranks recognized the talent he saw right away.

This young kid was far and away better than anyone else his age in the central area at the time. Drillon had picked him out early enough and no doubt had put the word out locally and abroad that he had discovered an outstanding player. Unfortunately, Drillon would only spend that one year in Grand Falls but his loss would be compensated with another new arrival from the mainland in the person of playing-coach Joe Byrne. Byrne would spend the rest of his life in Newfoundland, a career spanning some 40 years, his coaching influence happily split between the communities of Grand Falls and Bell Island. His influence on George Faulkner's career would be immediate and lasting.

In early September 1951, still eligible for high school hockey and more than ready for another run at the league championship, 17-year-old George Faulkner, second youngest in a family of seven children, five boys and two girls, found himself instead on his way to hockey tryouts in Quebec City. Coach Joe Byrne, from the nearby and much bigger town of Grand Falls, whose brother Frank owned the Junior "B" Quebec Citadelles, selected Faulkner and three other locals for the invitation to the Quebec tryouts. Faulkner came out of the high school league, while the other three – goalie Dougal Foote from Botwood, Tom Blackmore and Fred Sanger from Grand Falls – had completed their season at the more experienced junior hockey level. He'd scouted them carefully throughout the past season, remembering the impression they had made on coach Gordie Drillon a couple of years earlier.

Byrne was particularly taken by Faulkner. As impressed as he was with the playing level of all four teenagers, Byrne was more excited from the beginning by what he saw of this young kid's dominating play in the high school ranks. Byrne watched him play a few times in the local senior men's league as well that year, representing his hometown team of Bishop's Falls. Again, he was impressed. Faulkner continued to display the same talents at this more advanced level of the game, fitting in quite nicely game after game, despite his age. He was just 16 years old, but even at this juncture in his playing career he stood out, showed more promise than the others and, in Byrne's experience in these matters, just might be the one to make it.

The sendoff from home had been guarded, the family well aware of what lay ahead. Byrne was careful to advise them of the kind of realities he would soon encounter, the kind of competition the youngster would be facing in Quebec right from the outset. "He'll be going up against maybe 60–80 other kids, mostly from Quebec. Most of them have been on skates all their lives. The winters are so long up there that they play the game practically the whole year. These young buggers are damn good. I've seen enough of them to know. They live and breathe hockey. Always have. Like I said, they're good."

George Faulkner, as young as he was, knew the only real issue facing him was how well he would hold up when it came to his skating. He knew where he stood at home, at the high school level where he had just finished. He was clearly well above the rest. His hockey abilities, i.e., shooting, stickhandling and passing, told him the same. He was good, and this tryout in Quebec, as intimidating as it might be, did not overwhelm him. He was nervous, but keen enough not to let it get the better of him. "Wait and see," he thought. "I'll wait and see what they've got before I go off in any one direction on how good they might or might not be." One thing for sure, he recalls – with a touch of laughter – it would not be anything like the first time he skated on frozen spots of water around town with crushed tin cans attached to his boots. More to the point, he knew his own strengths when it came to what the Quebec league could offer.

Byrne's final observation to the Faulkner family that September was more hard-nosed than he might have intended, but it left no doubt in their minds as to the grind that was coming for the eager young teenager: "The camp lasts for about two weeks. They start cutting back the roster after the first week. Depending on how he does up there, he could be gone for the winter or he could be home in a week."

For most of the early 1950s the Quebec City Major Junior Hockey League (QMJHL) was made up of two divisions: Junior "A" and Junior "B." In reality, it was the older, more experienced Junior "A" which got most of the attention from both hockey scouts and local sports media. Junior "B" was considered the proving ground for the senior team, much like today's arrangement between the NHL and AHL. You were being groomed at the lower level for the important second year of hockey in Junior "A," when most players had turned 18 and were better able to withstand the pressures and intensity of the game at that level. George and his Newfoundland buddies managed to observe a few of the Junior "A" practices during the first week, and were immediately thrilled with the play of Camille Henry, Connie Broden, Marcel Paille, Charlie Hodge and many others – names they did not yet recognize, but whose stars were already burning brightly on the Quebec hockey scene.

In the third year of junior play, the league management began to look seriously at which players might be ready for the professional ranks. The decision at this stage was to sign prospects either to a professional contract with amateur status ("minor pro"), or professional in the fullest sense – meaning an incredible jump to one of six teams in the NHL at the time: Montreal, Toronto, Boston, Chicago, Detroit or New York. At such a young age, this remained the realm of the superstar only, the likes of Gordie Howe, Jean Beliveau or Henri "Pocket Rocket" Richard.

Today's selection system, though differing greatly in process, is based on the same specific, single criteria: talent. In the case of George Faulkner's future, it would turn out to be something more: a combination of talent and circumstance.

3

QUEBEC CITY

COACH JOE BYRNE, EVER A CAREFUL AND PRAGMATIC
fellow, had willingly offered to accompany the four young athletes to Quebec
City, a four- to five-day journey by rail, sea and road. Byrne was the proud owner
of a late-model Chevrolet and looked forward to the trip almost as much as the
kids themselves. Joe was the purser for the trip, financed entirely by the Quebec
Citadelles organization, and could be counted on to spend wisely, even with
someone else's money.

Shortly before leaving home, and after receiving the official invitation to
attend tryouts, Lester and Olive accompanied George on a special buying trip to
Riff's Department Store for new clothes: shirts, pants ("with the modern-day
24-inch cuffs"), a new raglan, complete with zippered lining ("everybody wore
a raglan like that back then"), and last of all, to complete his new "gentlemanly"
appearance, a new cap – complete with peak and all. There was never the like
of such grandeur in the Faulkner home before. "I was all dickied off, for sure,"
he would say.

The CNR transported Byrne's 1949 Chev on a flatcar as far as Port
aux Basques for the crossing on the newest gulf ferry, the M.V. *Cabot Strait*, a
two-year-old addition to the fleet. The flatcar rode several cars behind on the
same train and every time the train lurched or its cars bumped together in a
domino-effect pattern, Byrne would almost jump out of his seat, worried about
what might be happening just a few cars behind. Then there was the frightening
strain of climbing the infamous Gaff Topsails, a long series of uphill track known
for its winter blockages of snow. Even at this time of year, the Gaff Topsails

could often be a challenge to the aging steam locomotives in the Newfoundland rail system. On its run up this legendary section of rail in the very heart of the province, the train, lovingly referred to by the travelling public as "The Newfie Bullet," would be moving at its slowest, a tormenting dead-slow pace ("You could see the rust comin' on her"), and the butt of many fanciful stories because of it. "I think Joe suffered every foot of the climb on that trip," George laughs, "thinking the Chev might fall off, or get squashed, but nothing came of it. We finally got there in one piece, car and all."

The new ferry was launched shortly after the province's entry into Confederation in 1949. "The *Cabot Strait* was a beauty: modern, with the best of meals and accommodations. We thought we were in some fancy hotel somewhere." Shortly after the sailing began, however, and no longer in sight of the shores of home, a note of anxiety surfaced among the group. Someone mentioned the loss of the M.V. *Caribou* during a crossing in 1942.* "We got out into open water and it became kind of eerie, and the guys started talking about what happened to the *Caribou*," George recalls. "Even though the war was over, it wasn't that long ago; a lot of people on board still remembered what had happened, and the thought occurred to some that maybe those German subs were still lurking out there, in all that fog. You felt a long way from home once you got out in the Gulf."

However, the only thing to go overboard on the trip was George's new cap, the brown-sprinkled object with a fancy peak the family had bought for him a few days before. Maybe to offset the uneasy atmosphere the talk of the tragedy had caused, Dougal Foote, the fun-loving goalie from Botwood, grabbed it off George's head and tossed it overboard, all the while trying hard to control the laughter as they watched it float away in the fog.

Cape Breton, on the other side of the Gulf and a world away from the rugged Newfoundland coastline, was in full bloom that September. They say the season of autumn finds Cape Breton at its most beautiful, its hills and highlands flourishing in the late summer light. This September day was exactly like that. The land still held the heat of a long summer as the first touches of autumn colors

---

* The *Caribou* was torpedoed by a German submarine in October that year, with a loss of 137 passengers and crew.

began to show themselves.

The route from North Sydney would take them along the Bras d'Or Lakes, a picturesque run to Port Hastings at the other end of the island, and a quick crossing of the Strait of Canso by ferry into mainland Nova Scotia. Unlike the narrow gravel roads at home, they could now sail along on paved highways through the rest of Nova Scotia and New Brunswick, and from there on to Quebec City, following the panoramic shoreline of the St. Lawrence River the rest of the way. Certainly, it was a breathtaking introduction to the sheer enormity of their newly adopted homeland.

The first sight of Quebec City was overwhelming. To the eyes of an innocent kid from a town of two or three thousand people, the spectacle of what lay before him, a city whose population almost equaled that of his entire home province,* was breathtaking. First, there was the magnificence of its location along the St. Lawrence River. Despite what little experience he might have brought to these new surroundings, the striking contrast between the Exploits River back home – a mere 1,200 feet wide at Bishop's Falls – and the mighty St. Lawrence, more than one-half mile in width, as it moved past Quebec City, overwhelmed him. The magic and immensity of the river, like the city itself, was difficult to grasp.

For the first time George and his friends would see a strategic part of Canadian history in its real form. Their accommodation was within walking distance of the Plains of Abraham, Canada's national shrine to its French/English past, just about as authentically Canadian as it gets. The story of the two famous generals from the Battle of the Plains of Abraham, Wolfe and Montcalm, practically jumped out at them on a daily basis. "For some reason," George explained, "and from what little I remember of the details of this part of our history, I somehow always took a liking to Montcalm, more so than to Wolfe. Seems he was the more tragic figure of the two." Many Canadians would probably agree.

But for the next few days and weeks they would not be getting much interference from matters of history in their day-to-day affairs. There would be time for

---

* Quebec City's metropolitan area population at the time was about 300,000, Newfoundland's population about 360,000.

little else but hockey and hard work. The living arrangements for the group turned out to be quite comfortable, and proved to be only a short bus ride to the downtown area and the Quebec Colisée, where the camp was being held. They were set up in a modern tourist home, an off-season arrangement the club had made for them, complete with their own rooms, home-cooked meals ("almost as good as home"), for as long as their stay would last – at the moment, an unknown and anxious prospect for each one of them.

The only equipment they brought from home was their skates – everything else would be provided by the team. George had brought along a new pair of Tackaberry skates, second only to the more popular CCMs, which only a few kids could afford. The 'Tacks' were a gift donation from his buddies on the Bishop's Falls hockey team and would put him on a par with everyone else when it came to skating. The rest was up to him.

Hockey sticks were also a precious and expensive commodity back home, even at 75 cents a piece. George couldn't believe he'd have his own selection of sticks throughout the tryouts. "Nothing like that in Bishop's. We'd have one stick for almost the whole winter. If you suddenly broke a stick in the middle of some big game, you'd skate to the bench like a bat out of hell to grab one from one of the guys – skate by the bench in a panic and reach for a stick – any kind of stick. The guys would get such a fright they were going to lose the only stick they had, they'd all pull back, and leave you just standing there, 'til the coach slapped one of them in the back of the head and simply pointed. That's how precious a stick was then."

The question of money was a very simple affair – they were given a bi-weekly allowance, in cash, of twenty-five dollars. Since every other facet of their trip was covered by the organization, including room and board and meals, the allowance would be more than enough to see them through. It was spending money only, the boys were told, if they ever got the time to spend it. They considered the generous offer more like a small fortune.

The most unnerving piece of news they would get before practices began was the selection format to be used during camp. Each of the four cringed when told that a roster would be posted on the dressing room blackboard at the end of each day, listing the names of those who were invited to return next day. If at the end of a day your name was missing from that roster, you knew you were on your way home. For George Faulkner, as well as others, it made them anxious from the outset, even before they stepped on the ice for that first and now even more intimidating practice: "You can imagine how nervous we all were to hear that. There'd be no chance for a second look, no chance to explain that you'd had a bad day at practice or weren't feeling well, and you'd do better tomorrow. Nothing. Just pack your bags. It was frightening at the end of each day to sit in the dressing room and wait for that posting and wonder if you were still part of the camp."

The team held two practices a day, morning and afternoon, after which they were free to socialize, mostly taking in a movie downtown, and the odd treat of a coke and burger. Unlike the accepted practice of many of today's young athletes, alcohol, in any form, was unheard of. In any case, they soon learned there was little time for anything else but practice. The drills were gruelling, the scrimmages ("more like skirmishes") were tough and would only get tougher as the number of recruits got smaller each day and the competition improved accordingly. Even though it was always a relief to see your name on the daily posting, you felt bad for the guys who didn't make it, especially if you thought you were responsible in any way. "In the one-on-one drills – trying to beat a defenceman for a shot on goal and knowing that this wasn't supposed to happen – you felt bad when you got around a guy and afterwards saw the scared look on his face as he skated past the coach on his way back to the bench."

"Just part of the natural selection process," one coach explained. George had no idea what he was talking about.

To make matters worse, the day finally came when it got close to home.

Day after day, Faulkner's name continued to appear on the roster. The others, however, Blackmore, Foote and Sanger, managed to survive the cut for only a few days. They weren't really surprised. At 19 years old, they would be starting their last year of junior play and could see for themselves how the younger crop, even now, were that much more advanced than themselves. There was simply no time available to make up the difference. For them, the invitation to the tryouts had come a little too late. Still, the trip had been worth it – every minute of the experience would be remembered for a lifetime, and they could always consider themselves as having had a shot – no matter how small – at the "big time." Not everyone back home could say that.

Before leaving for home the day after they got the bad news, the three friends got together to say a brief farewell to the last Newfoundland hopeful. "You're the one, now, George. It's all on you. We know you'll do okay – for heaven's sake, you can skate backwards faster than most of them can forwards. See you back home at Christmas."

Dougal Foote, as a kind of parting shot, concluded the parting of the ways: "George, they told us they're going to fly us home; only for that I'd have a look crossing the Gulf for that fancy cap of yours."

With the loss of his three buddies from home, it took George a while to adjust to his new situation. The group had shared a lot of good times together – the trip from home, the training camp – even the little socializing they did kept them together at the end of each day of training. He was glad, however, they saw the age difference, even though it was only a year or so, as the biggest factor in their not making it; but it still felt awkward to see them have to leave the way they did. It would be the first of many disappointments to come his way in this new world that lay ahead of him.

He soon learned his new roommate would be Leo Amadio, a kid who had hopped a ride with them to Quebec from the small Cape Breton community of Donkin. Amadio, it turned out, would stay with the Citadelles organization that year, ensuring the two would remain friends – if not teammates – for the next few years in Quebec hockey circles.* Another hurdle was now out of the way, leaving very little to distract him from the day-to-day routine of continuing to work out with the squad.

He was already feeling stronger, and skating better, and as the camp routine wore on and more and more players disappeared from the dreaded blackboard lists, he began to feel more confident in his chances.

George wasn't aware that a highly encouraging report had already appeared in the Grand Falls *Advertiser* of October 25, about two weeks into the camp. Joe Byrne reported home that Citadelles coach and camp supervisor, Phil Watson, liked what he saw in young Faulkner:

> Watson ... predicts that in a few years he'll be playing pro hockey ...
> Faulkner was rated the best prospect in camp and will be heard
> from in a few years.

At the same time, George himself slowly began to realize he was every bit as

---

* Amadio was the younger brother of Neil Amadio, a semi-pro player who became a dominant figure in Newfoundland hockey, especially in the Grand Falls area. Leo would be selected to play Junior "B" that year with an opposing side – St. Patrick's High School – in the same league.

good as the rest of the fellows in the fundamentals of the game. The daily roster posting – still intimidating to a point – was finally beginning to lose much of its meaning.

It began to look as if he might really be here to stay.

The final posting came at the end of the third week of training camp. Routines changed considerably as the number of players became more manageable. Practices were longer and there was a lot more scrimmage time as the coaches experimented with different line possibilities. George played centre and left wing for most of the time and was getting as much ice time and personal attention as any of the others. At one practice, he noticed Phil Watson in the stands and figured something important was about to happen. Maybe this was the last "look" the head coach needed before making the final cut. "I turned on the burners when I caught a glimpse of old Phil up there. He coached the "A" team and oversaw our squad once in awhile. He scared the hell out of all of us whenever he was around and we hadn't seen him in a while."

It turned out George was right. That afternoon, at the end of a particularly long practice session, freshly showered, he quickly made his way to the now-familiar blackboard area, more anxious on this afternoon than ever. There it was, in bold if unsteady lettering: FINAL CUT. His name was still there.

Of all possible coaches young George Faulkner could have played under as a novice in this new world of big-time hockey, it would be his misfortune, at least in the early goings, to fall under the wing of "Fiery Phil" Watson, the legendary New York Ranger right winger and holder of two Stanley Cup championship rings. Watson could intimidate the entire hockey establishment: players, owners, referees, and the league management itself. He was a known fighter, hard on his players – young and old – but he knew hockey and gained the highest respect of players throughout his long, often belligerent, coaching career. In one historic disagreement during the 1952-53 Junior "A" playoffs, Watson disputed a goal by the Montreal Junior Canadiens and rather than settle it by admitting that he had overreacted to the disputed call, pulled the team out of the playoffs, then out of the league altogether, and went on to join the playoffs for the Memorial Cup instead.

Luckily, George saw the better side of him right away. Whatever else, this guy knew the game and there was a lot to be learned from him. As it happened, Watson's role with the Citadelles' organization that year was as head coach of both "A" and "B" teams, but he was directly involved only with the "A" team, meaning they wouldn't have Fiery Phil looking over their shoulders at every turn.

It turned out that the Junior "B" team, because of youth and inexperience, did not get anything near the media attention of its senior complement. Individual and team records, even team rosters, do not exist for that division. What remains in the books is playoff history only. The league consisted of four teams: Quebec Citadelles, Montmorency Falls, Montmagny and Quebec St. Patrick's, a mixed high school/junior level team also owned by Frank Byrne. St. Patrick's would be the home team of George's new friend from Cape Breton, Leo Amadio, that first year. The two would become linemates further on in their young careers.

George managed to get home that Christmas, almost a surprise visit, since no one had expected to see him before the end of the hockey season in April. The high school hockey league was still in operation at home and it happened that the two main competitors in the league – Bishop's Falls and Grand Falls Academy – were scheduled to play the final game before the Christmas break. Younger brother Alex, a 16-year-old at the time, had become the team spokesman, not to mention its leading scorer, and wasted no time trying to convince George to suit up for the game against Grand Falls. The reason for trying to get him to play stemmed from a rather odd situation with a Grand Falls player. Cec Thomas, the best player on the Grand Falls squad, had left school just before Christmas and was now working at the mill. Technically, he should have been ineligible to play, but word got around that, somehow, through some kind of loophole, he was going to be in the lineup for the crucial game against Bishop's.

"Cec was a real good player," according to George, "and would have made a big difference to the outcome of the game; so brother Alex, not to be outdone, decided I should be allowed to play as well, since I was taking a course or two in Quebec – a plain case of 'sauce for the goose being sauce for the gander.'"

Few people knew George Faulkner was home for Christmas, and no one in Grand Falls would know until he was the last player to step on the ice for the warm-up exercise for the game that day. Alex had him stay in the dressing

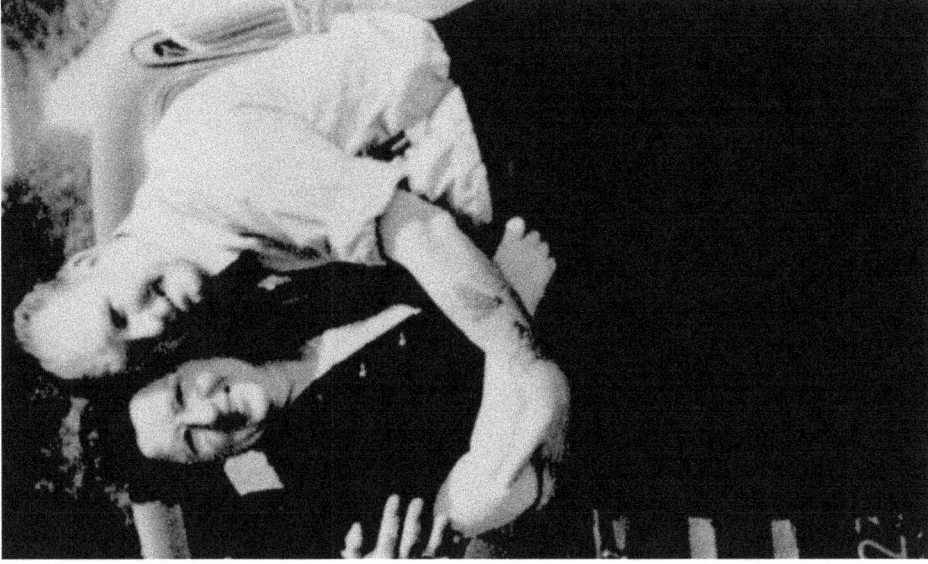

HOCKEY WAS NOT HIS ONLY LOVE.
Lester and Olive Faulkner at home in Bishop's
Falls, 1956.

THE LINDAHL FAMILY. Fourteen-year-old Svea (far right) would become grandmother to the Faulkner clan. "Grandpa" Lindahl was killed in an industrial accident at Bishop's Falls in 1918.

THE RINK AT ROUNDHOUSE COVE. The three older Faulkners (front, L to R – Alex, George, Lindy) are seen sporting their favourite NY Rangers jerseys.

GEORGE, AGE 10, with boots in hand, about to start his hockey day on the Exploits River. The background shows the Bishop's Falls railway trestle.

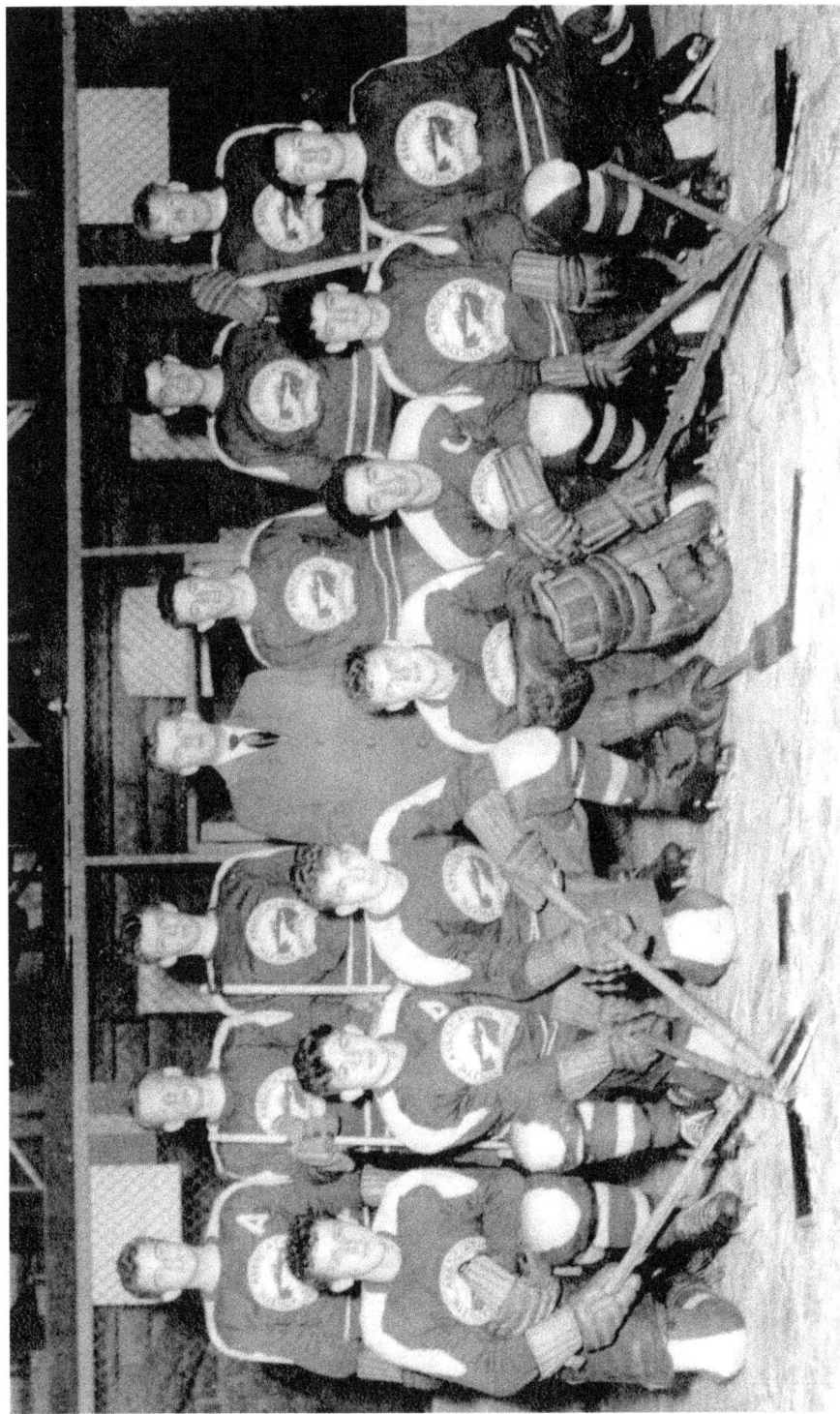

NEWFOUNDLAND JUNIOR CHAMPS, 1948. George, 15, (standing, last on the right), along with fellow tryouts to Quebec, Tom Blackmore (standing, first left), and goalie Dougal Foote. Coach Joe Byrne is shown with his first winning team from Grand Falls.

THE FLYING FAULKNERS TAKE ON THE PROFESSIONALS. In an exhibition game played in Grand Falls during a tour in 1957, an all-star collection from the Quebec leagues got the surprise of their young lives when George's four brothers joined him in a third-period exchange of players against the Quebecers. The roof almost lifted off the Grand Falls Stadium. (L to R: Alex (21), Lindy (26), George (23), (Lester Faulkner), Seth (19) and 14-year-old Jack.)

room until the Bishop's Falls team –all seven of them – were already out there. "When I hit the ice and started to skate around with the rest of the team, someone spotted me, and the whole Grand Falls team – a full squad of 18 or so players – just stopped and stood there. They couldn't believe what they were seeing." Their next reaction was to skate en masse to the team's bench to protest. The long and short of it was that there was no game played that day. "Neither team would agree to allow myself or Cec to play and the game was cancelled outright. We went back to the dressing room, changed outfits, and went home. Alex said afterwards they could have beaten Grand Falls either way."

After a first place finish in a 24-game season, the Citadelles went on to win the league championship, ousting St. Patrick's four games to two in the semi-finals, and then defeating the Quebec Aces four games to none in the finals. They would go on to represent the Quebec City League in the provincial finals against Montreal NDG Monarchs (Mount Royal Junior League), Montreal Cinderella (Laurentienne Junior League), and Cap-de-la-Madeleine (Eastern Provincial League).

The Citadelles became Provincial Junior "B" Champions that year, defeating Cap-de-la-Madeleine in the finals in straight games, outscoring them 11-6 in a two-game series.

They had made "Fiery Phil," the tempestuous figure who had appeared at so many of their practices – it seemed out of nowhere – a very happy man.

George felt that he had had more than a satisfactory year with the Citadelles and had played more hockey than he could ever imagine possible. At 18, he was in peak form, with two more years of junior level play still ahead of him. He had satisfied himself and the coaching staff that he belonged. Everything seemed to add up to a busy summer back in Bishop's Falls and a return to Quebec for a second time in September. For a number of reasons, it did not work out quite that way.

For one thing, at the conclusion of the season there was no communication with team owner Frank Byrne or any of the coaches, including "Fiery Phil." They were given no indication where their future might be with the organization, or what immediate prospects might be ahead for the 1952-53 season. There was no team meeting at the end to underscore the season just finished, no outlay of plans for change, no new strategies for the year ahead. Nothing. It was simply like any other day at the rink. The players wrapped up the season by getting a ticket home and nothing else. It seemed the next year would be like the last: wait for the call and begin tryouts all over again.

George prepared to return home, unceremoniously it seemed, but still very eager to enjoy a summer of playing soccer and doing some part-time work repairing gravel roads – a government "make work" program of the time.

The ticket home was via Trans-Canada Airlines, his first flight. Not that it mattered, but it turned out to be "an all-night milk run" – Quebec City to Moncton, Halifax, Sydney, Stephenville and Gander, aboard the revered and ageless DC-3 aircraft. "Next to making the team and scoring that first goal, that flight was one of the highlights of the year."

George Faulkner's hockey experience in Quebec would see him quickly move allegiances away from favourite NHL teams he had adopted from childhood – Toronto and New York – although he could never figure why he cheered for New York. The change began during this first year away from home when his interest turned largely to what was happening in Quebec hockey, especially, as one would expect, how the "big club," Les Habs, prospered each time out. It was part of the big dream.

A few years before the Canadiens began their five-year reign of Stanley Cup Championships (1956-60), they had had their problems with inconsistent performances and frequent, sometimes very big, turnovers in their roster.

The 1948 season stands out. The team finished in fifth place, out of the playoffs, with a won-lost-tied record of 20-29-11 in the old 60-game format. Coach Dick Irvin would begin the next season with ten new faces in the lineup and end the year in second place but with no Stanley Cup.

The 1950-51 season introduced two brilliant new rookies to the team – Bernie "Boom Boom" Geoffrion and superstar Jean Beliveau, both just 19 years old. Geoffrion stayed with the club, while Beliveau remained a holdout for another two years before signing a pro contract. As the old Montreal guard slowly declined with injuries and retirements, a new breed of player would take over, a building process that would create in a few short years the most successful organization ever in hockey.

However, there was still a small mountain or two to climb, in the form of the other two dominant clubs in the league, Detroit and Toronto. In the span of years from 1948 to 1955, the Detroit Red Wings would win the Stanley Cup four times, Toronto would claim three, and Montreal just one, in 1953.

George Faulkner's entry into the Quebec hockey world in 1951 came at a time of much re-organization at the top level in Montreal, the faces of its players changing yearly until 1956 when it would complete its turn-around, giving the team a stability that would last into the next decade.

4

DECISION

FOR A KID ON HIS WAY TO A CAREER IN PRO HOCKEY, it might have seemed like a peculiar decision.

After making the Citadelles' lineup at age 17 and playing through a successful season at the Junior "B" level in Quebec City, at the end of the summer Faulkner decided he would stay home for the 1952-53 year. "I was just 18 years old and I was offered a permanent job at the mill in Grand Falls. A permanent job in those days was a big deal. It was also a job that paid well, and I couldn't pass it up. Hockey, after all, was still a big question mark."

For some strange and unknown reason, he was not aware at the time that the Citadelles wanted him back. The word would certainly have come down to his long-time mentor, Joe Byrne, who was responsible for all hockey matters in Grand Falls and whose brother still owned the Quebec Citadelles. When he learned of Faulkner's decision to stay home for the year, he obviously let the matter rest there. He knew young George had been hired full-time by the mill, and with the prospect of having him available to play with the Grand Falls All-stars – in fact, to play on the same line with himself and playing-coach Wes Trainor – it might have made sense to Byrne, in the interests of a good hockey year at home, to say nothing. Politics, even in the game of hockey, it seems, gives no quarter.

Apart from what might have been in Quebec that year, there was still plenty of hockey at home, and at the provincial senior level, and playing on a line with two ex-pros would give him a different perspective on the game and plenty of challenges coming from their individual styles and exceptional abilities. Both

Trainor and Byrne were still in great playing form, leaving little doubt that the year would not be a total loss, certainly not from what was to be gained from the experience of playing with these two. All that was missing, he remembers thinking, was the influence of "Fiery Phil" Watson.

His job at the mill paid forty-three dollars per week – a good salary back then and it was permanent, with opportunities to progress within the industry. In the beginning he was assigned "on the broke" – cleaning up paper breaks at the huge drying machines. A large piece of wire mesh would take the wet end of newly ground pulp from the grinding room to a huge drying machine, where it would begin its paper run. It was the "broker's" job to supervise the operation in case of any paper breaks, which had to be corrected immediately. "You only had seconds to get to the machine. If you had a break and didn't get to it in time, if it got away from you, you'd have an explosion of paper on the floor within seconds. That could mean a full day's clean-up." Not quite the pre-game leisure time of today's athletes.

Decision made, George Faulkner settled in to life in Grand Falls, a full-time position at the local paper mill, and a new challenge in the game he loved.

At age 18, standing 5'9 ½", and hardly above welterweight status at 152 pounds, he was ready to unleash upon the local hockey scene a singular talent more advanced than anyone remotely expected. The years of playing at Roundhouse Cove on the Exploits River, and the impressive learning experience gained from his year in Quebec had placed him at the pinnacle of his game. They were about to pay off handsomely – especially for his hometown of Bishop's Falls.

The local club league got underway in November, with four teams and a schedule of 12 games per team. The teams – Bishop's Falls (the "Woodsmen"), Guards (last year's winners), CLB and Hawks – comprised players from all over the area, with an "open" player selection process. Bishop's Falls would include, once again, the three Faulkner brothers: Lindy, age 20; George, 18; and Alex, a youthful 16-year-old, still eligible for the high school ranks. Playing-coach Joe Byrne, at 31, joined the squad and played on a line with George and another skilled forward, Dave Greene.

A quick look at league statistics that year tells all:

AFTER 4 GAMES	GOALS	ASSISTS	POINTS
George Faulkner	11	6	17
Alex Faulkner	5	5	10
Lindy Faulkner	3	6	9
AFTER 6 GAMES			
George Faulkner	14	8	22
Dave Greene	11	5	16
Alex Faulkner	7	8	15
AFTER 12 GAMES			
George Faulkner	27	17	44
Dave Greene	10	17	27
Alex Faulkner	13	11	24

The team would go undefeated for the season, a feat never before accomplished in league play. In the traditional year-end exhibition game between the winners and a team made up of league all-stars, the Bishop's crew continued their dominance. The squad won easily, 5-2, with George contributing three goals and one assist.

The playoffs for the Herder Memorial Trophy, a provincial championship series going back to 1935, began in March. Competitors came from east and west of the island: Corner Brook, Buchans, Grand Falls, Gander, Bell Island, and St. John's (usually represented by one of its senior "club" teams).

The semi-finals against a poor squad from Gander proved to be a wipeout, as expected. In back-to-back wins, Grand Falls outscored Gander 22-0. Faulkner contributed six points: three goals and three assists. The finals, against perennial winners Buchans Miners, would be a different affair and the lads from the Grand Falls squad knew it. They were aware as well that, in nearly 20 years of competition, they had never won the Herder. Buchans, winners of the title for three years running, were long-shot favourites, as usual.

The series would be a best-of-three affair, played in Grand Falls in mid-March. Attendance at the small Grand Falls arena for the series would soar to nearly six thousand, the highest attendance ever recorded up to that time.

The Buchans Miners lineup included a starting line of three players from PEI: Al Carver, Willie Robinson and Mark Kelly – a given match-up against the Grand Falls first line of George Faulkner, Joe Byrne and Dave Green. For the first time in a long while, the outcome of a series was uncertain. Buchans sported other great names that year, many of them remembered to this day as legends of the old Newfoundland game: defenceman Bill Scott; Hugh Wadden; the Mullins brothers – Ron and Al; Jimmy Hornell; Cape Breton's wonderful goalie of the time, "Sham" McInnis; and a skillful, free-spirited player George remembered well. "George Pike was one helluva hockey player. Talent to burn. He got away with a lot because he was always a kind of individual playmaker and not much of a team man. He'd remind you of the kind of player Ted Gillies of St. Bon's* was – a dipsy-doodler – very much an individualist. If they tried to play like that anywhere else, they'd be killed."

The Grand Falls lineup had more than its share of talent and well-known stars on the provincial scene as well: "Bucky" Hannaford, Al Folkes, Ray Marshall, Wes Trainor, Joe Byrne, and former teammates of Faulkner's – Fred Sanger and Dougal Foote.

The series was everything it was expected to be – except for the outcome. Grand Falls won the Herder in two straight: 6-4 and 4-1. It was the most exciting hockey the area had ever seen.

The season came to an end with the series against Buchans. In all, the team had played 22 games, including exhibitions, losing only once, to a team from North Sydney. George had played in all 22 games, and amassed an impressive 36 points (21 goals, 15 assists). For the full 1952-53 season, including play at the club level, he had played 34 games, scored a total of 48 goals, and set up 32 others. Coupled with the two championships recorded in Quebec the year before, the Herder

---

* Gillies was a star athlete for St. Bon's Bluegolds, a club team from the local league in St John's. The team represented the city for many years in provincial competition, winning the Herder Memorial Trophy a total of ten times.

victory marked four consecutive championships for the young hockey star in just two years.

He was voted the senior league's MVP, and remembers receiving a new Alpacama overcoat as part of the award. "That was some overcoat," George recalled with a laugh. "It was donated by Cohen's Store in Grand Falls. It was such a long and heavy thing, I must've looked like a young Al Capone in his Chicago days. I couldn't wear it out. In the end, I had to give it away."

The question of whether he would be ready for his final year of junior hockey in Quebec, or anywhere else, had been clearly answered. All he needed now was the opportunity, and, as it happened, that opportunity was not long in coming.

5

"THEY WANT YOU BACK"

AS THE SEASONS COME AND GO ALONG THE EXPLOITS
River, the passing of winter, with its exciting invitation to hockey and life in the
great outdoors, is easily compensated for by the beauty of its summer, and, in
some years, a touch of spring that can be felt stirring along its shores.

> My grandfather had a boat on the river, a single piston boat, and he
> used to take us up the river, and then across the river, up near
> the depot where the woods operation started. This was just
> above Bishop's, on the other side of the river. We'd go up in early
> morning and not get back 'til dark. The trouting was unbelievable.

The half-hour run to the depot on the other side of the river was followed by a
day's hiking to the interior, to places like Tolt Brook and Fork Lakes. The
Faulkner boys and their grandfather walked most of the day, moving inland from
place to place in search of the right 'spot'. "When we'd get back home, we'd all
have full baskets of slivers, enough trout for a week at the house."

After a winter of hockey activity such as he'd just had – the travel, the
practices, the bumps and grinds of each game, and the mental fatigue that came
with it – it felt good to get away from it all and spend time on the river – a
return to the past and the good family times they had shared while growing up
there. Sometimes, just an afternoon swim would serve the same purpose.

The responsibility he carried at the mill was another high-pressure
situation, another good reason to escape to the river. The role of "broker" kept
you on your toes throughout each working day. There was no time to be idle

41

when the huge paper machines were rolling. It was definitely a young man's job, but even so, it was tiring and exacting work. He had been told many times, and the thought was always there: in this work, catastrophe was just the blink of an eye away.

Still, a day on the river could be a cure for that, too.

At the end of the working day and on weekends, life in the small community moved on like that in many others – a time of rest and solitude for some, a time for plenty of outdoor activities for others. Sports was still high on the list, in the form of soccer, which turned out to be almost as popular as hockey. Music, too, became a favourite pastime. Old railway boxcars, with almost perfect acoustics, became hangouts for George and a few of his musical friends. He played mandolin at the time, then switched to guitar, which became a lifelong hobby. "Sometimes we'd gather on Tobin's front veranda with the Tobins and O'Keefes for jam sessions – always with an eye to the girls, of course." Bonfire nights were the most popular events of the time, as they probably were everywhere in the 1950s, but not everyone had an Exploits River at their doorstep. Series of fires along the shores of the Exploits were commonplace on the long summer nights.

After turning 18, that summer saw him behind the wheel of the family pick-up truck, as usual, a brand new Chevy. It later became his means of winter transportation back and forth to hockey games and practices in Grand Falls, and always with a truckload of players and equipment on board. The Faulkner home became the transportation hub for both sport and socializing, with George at the centre of it all.

By late summer, Bishop's Falls began to think hockey once again, and perhaps look ahead to a repeat of the achievements of last year. The hockey team had been the talk of the small town all winter long. But the league itself, and in particular the larger community of Grand Falls, faced the difficult question of how to handle the dominance displayed by the Bishop's squad; i.e., what to do with those Faulkners? The league needed more team balance to keep competitive, and the only way to do that was to shake things up and, hopefully, get everyone to agree to do what was best for the league. There was still plenty of talent around from last year's lineups. The question was how best to use it.

On a warm afternoon near the end of the summer, Joe Byrne drove down the highway to Bishop's Falls, to the Faulkner home, thoughts of the oncoming hockey season foremost on his mind. As always, it was an informal visit, but on this occasion it carried a certain, almost official, air: a business call but it had nothing to do with the local hockey scene. George remembered that both his parents were present.

"They want you back," Byrne said.

The Faulkner family had no idea this was coming, as startled at the news as they were momentarily excited by it. The idea of returning to Quebec was never far from George's mind. He hadn't really given up on the prospect of another try at making the NHL someday, and the season just past had made believers of a great many other people as well. They needed little more in the way of proof of what this kid could do. Again, and for the second time in his young working life, it had come down to the question of quitting a job at home and gambling on a tough road ahead, with maybe little compensation in the end.

"Would you give it one last try?" Byrne asked. He was not insistent or pushing the matter. He knew full well the implications of the decision. He had been through all of this himself just a few years before.

In truth, there was some hesitation on George's part, but not much. "I wanted to go. That was the heart of it." And his parents agreed. The decision was just that simple.

There were more formalities to his venture this time around but thankfully fewer unknowns: he would have to sign a "B" Form, thereby becoming the property of the New York Rangers. The Junior "A" Quebec Citadelles was a farm team of the Rangers, and by signing he would become their property for the foreseeable future.

The move to the Ranger organization should not have been surprising, since both Joe Byrne and Phil Watson were long affiliated with the New York team, and the Citadelles team owner, Frank Byrne, was under contract with them as well. The signing became a simple formality: George signed on, received a cheque from the Rangers for one hundred dollars, and was told that from now on he would play the game according to Canadian Amateur Hockey Association (CAHA) rules. "The minute I signed and took that cheque meant the only place I could legally play outside of the CAHA was back home in Newfoundland. We weren't part of the CAHA at the time." Little did he realize back then that he was entering an angry and tangled world of corporate hockey:

outright ownershipof players by management, no representation, no recourse in disputed matters, minimum salary scale, and no pension. Even for established NHL players, these concerns were still years in the future.*

One of George's first impressions of this second camp was the number of things that had changed in the Quebec Junior League in the past year. The loose, impersonal style associated with the way things were run at the "B" level was a thing of the past.

The training camp routine was much the same except that the anxiety caused by the daily listing of blackboard names was gone, at least for him.

The hard work regimen was still the same, and the daily schedule, the drills and scrimmages, were all there. Having already signed on with the club, there was a noticeable difference in the way he was treated as an individual. There was a more personal rapport with management and coaches. Hanging around the dressing room before and after each practice, George felt more a part of the organization, and it helped his play and his attitude toward the club considerably. The successes at home against older and often more formidable opponents, both in local competition and provincial play, had not only shown where his talents stood in terms of last year's competition, but, in fact, that he had improved on them at every turn.

Things looked good. Even the continued presence of coach Phil Watson on the bench, as demanding and bullying as ever, did not have the same bite anymore.

The most significant change came within the league structure itself. There were now two teams representing Quebec City: the Quebec Frontenacs and the original Quebec Citadelles. Each one had a different owner, and each was assigned to playing in a different league. The Citadelles had been switched to the Ontario Junior League, but were still the property of the New York Rangers; the Frontenacs became the latest acquisition of the Montreal Canadiens organization and would play in the Quebec Junior League. Ironically, the two would never

* Detroit's Ted Lindsay became the prime mover of the Players' Association to establish a "union" and was later joined by Montreal's Doug Harvey. Some demands were not met until 1958, and the union itself was not established until 1967. For their efforts, both Lindsay and Harvey were traded off like damaged goods to other teams in the league.

meet in league competition.

The new setup was a world entirely new to George Faulkner:

> We were on the road a lot that year for the first time, traveling by train or bus to Galt, Guelph, St. Catharines, Hamilton and Toronto. Toronto had two teams in this league – the Toronto Marlies and St. Mike's. Both played in Maple Leaf Gardens. That was a real change for us, playing in the holy shrine of the Leafs, much bigger even than the Quebec Colisée, which was still our home turf. I remember I was lucky enough in our first game to score two goals in the Gardens against the Marlies in front of seven or eight thousand people.

The tour would take them on the road for two weeks at a stretch. It gave him the feeling of being a professional for the first time. It was the real world of Junior "A": traveling throughout Ontario, staying in hotels, obeying team dress codes, and playing in front of thousands of fans in big arenas everywhere. It had all the markings of life, as they say, "in the big time."

The annual Christmas tour that year began in early December and would turn out to be a major turning point for everyone connected with the Citadelles organization.

At some point on the trip, word got around that sent shockwaves throughout the team and its coaches. They learned that the Quebec Frontenacs had bought their team, but no one in authority would confirm it. "Watson had to know but wouldn't tell us. We figured something would give when we finished the circuit." George was right. After arriving back home in Quebec, the team was fêted to a special dinner downtown at a place called *The Spaghetti House* and given certain details of the sale, but little was revealed about future plans. It was "the future plans" part of the evening that kept everyone guessing. It was made clear, however, that the two teams would be blended into one, and a voting process to elect one coach would be held in the morning.

Beyond that, all they knew was that the vote would be by secret ballot and, come morning, one of the two established coaches and one full roster of players would be gone.

Even though they had never met in league competition, making it impossible to judge them under fire, the two teams were noticeably different in depth and character. The Citadelles had been around much longer, had won championships at the local and provincial level, and were once again on their way to a winning season. Then there was the "take-no-prisoners" coaching style (a highly successful one) of Phil Watson. His record as player and coach was more than noteworthy. It was no surprise then that the first vote – to elect the new team's coach – would go unanimously to the older, if not meaner, Watson. Despite a reputation for his jarring coaching style, the youthful Citadelles saw beneath all that and instead recognized the man's talent before anything else. The first issue facing the new team was resolved without dispute.

As George recalled, the management of the two teams got together the next day to select the new team from a roster of about 40 players. It turned out that they chose only two players from the Frontenacs, goalkeeper Jacques Marcotte and winger Guy Rousseau,* and nearly all members of the Citadelles. In effect, the new Quebec Frontenacs became the now-defunct Citadelles, with Faulkner certainly among them. The move also meant a return to the Quebec Major Junior Hockey League (QMJHL) and away from the Ontario Hockey Association (OHA), where they had started the season. "Other than that, we just continued on with the schedule in Junior "A," still with an eye on making it to the Memorial Cup, the top prize in junior hockey in Canada." The teams they would face in the new league would include the popular Montreal Junior Canadiens, farm team of their big brothers in the NHL. Neither George Faulkner nor the other members of the Quebec Citadelles knew at the time that the entire deal had been brokered by the Montreal Canadiens. The organization now owned the two top junior teams in the province, and both would serve as the proving ground for its future NHL plans.

The exceptions to the matter of player ownership would be those players, including Faulkner, who had earlier signed with other NHL teams – the so-called B Form he had signed through Joe Byrne before leaving home that summer. Whether he realized it or not, he was still the property of the New York Rangers.

---

* Rousseau was the older brother of Bobby Rousseau, a Montreal Canadiens star in the 1960s.

The new Quebec Provincial Junior A Hockey League (QPJHL) would include the Montreal Junior Canadiens, Trois Rivières Reds, Montreal Junior Royals, Jonquière Marquis and the newly formed Quebec Frontenacs. On paper, the Canadiens looked impressive, with several future NHLers heading the roster: Henri Richard, Phil Goyette, Andre Pronovost, Claude Provost, Reggie Fleming, Forbes Kennedy, Scotty Bowman, and coach Sam Pollock. True to form, the Juniors would claim first place in league standings, winning 44 of the 55 games played. Second, with 31 wins, were the Quebec Frontenacs. The semi-finals would see the Junior Canadiens beat Trois Rivières four games to none, with a goal differential of 27-7. Quebec would oust the Montreal Junior Royals that year in semi-final play with an equally impressive four-game sweep, outscoring them 32-8. The two best teams in the league, Montreal and Quebec, would meet in a home-and-home, best-of-seven finals, as expected.

The way the 1953-54 junior season had gone, with the loss of the Citadelles and the sudden Montreal take-over, the Frontenacs were probably thinking the worst of outcomes when the finals came around. There was no question that the senior Canadiens club favoured its junior counterpart against them. The name Henri Richard, the Rocket's outstanding younger brother and already bearing the nickname of "Pocket Rocket," was on every tongue in Quebec already. Everyone was asking the obvious question: Was he even better than the "Rocket"? The team had finished 13 games ahead of the Frontenacs in regular season play, accumulating 24 more points and scoring 70 more goals in the process. In George Faulkner's mind, however, there were only thoughts of an earlier game against the Junior Canadiens that season when he scored three goals against them – on their home ice at the Montreal Forum.

Not surprisingly, the junior finals would see sellout crowds at both the Forum in Montreal and the Colisée in Quebec City.

The outcome, however, proved to be a huge embarrassment to Sam Pollock and his Junior Canadiens, and a monumental comeback victory for Phil Watson's Quebec Frontenacs. The Frontenacs swept the Canadiens in four straight games, including the two home games at the Forum, in what must have been further humiliation for the team. In game three, George scored the winning goal and had two assists in the team's 4-2 victory. The last game of the series, a 3-1 victory, had Guy Rousseau score all three goals before a sellout crowd at the Colisée of seventeen thousand. Overall, the Frontenacs outscored the Canadiens 14-6, leading an overexcited coach Phil Watson to sum up the series this way: "I'm still dreaming. Imagine winning four straight against Canadiens. After we won the first one at the Forum, I was figuring on taking the series in six games, but never in four." The jubilant Quebec Frontenacs' next move would be on to the Eastern Canada Memorial Cup playoffs.*

The NHL Entry Draft, first held in Montreal in 1963, has become a TV spectacular in recent years, comparable to an Academy Awards night: glamorous surroundings, pre-draft shirt-and-tie affairs, unlimited press coverage (beginning days before the event itself), lengthy interviews which often include player histories, contract-signing, sweater-wearing ceremonies with family and friends looking on – all directed at selecting the latest crop of NHL hockey stars from junior, collegiate and European leagues. The selection process is anything but a straightforward affair. Starting with the top draft pick and moving on to the last of two hundred or more prospects for 30 teams, the draft is a day-long process, and maybe months in preparation. It has become one of the most anticipated highlights of the hockey year.

At the end of their junior careers, in the spring of 1954, George Faulkner's generation encountered none of that, not so much as a hint of what the future might hold for them. Publicity of any kind was unheard of. It was an accepted part of the process in those years: no glamour, no spotlights and no contracts, professional or otherwise, until you were contacted by one of the NHL farm teams. Even then, there would only be an *invitation* to more tryouts before anything became final. You still had to "make" the team. In fact, the end of the 1953-54 season was an exact repeat of two years before: when the last game was played, you'd pack up your bags, head home, and wait and see.

Before leaving Quebec City and heading back to another summer road job in Bishop's Falls, George managed to meet briefly with coach Phil Watson who had taken a sudden interest in his career. Watson told him he could probably get him a spot in the QPHL (Quebec Professional Hockey League) which featured teams like the Quebec Aces, Montreal Royals and Shawinigan Falls Cataracts. He made it clear that there was nothing guaranteed. It turned out, with some irony,

---

* The team closed out the year by winning the first round of the Memorial Cup playoffs against a team from the Maritimes, before losing to the eventual Memorial Cup winners, St. Catharines Teepees, four games to two.

that not only was it not guaranteed, but the meeting became the last contact he would ever have with Watson.

It would be near the end of summer before he would get any kind of official word from the team, and even then it would have a surprise in store for him. Though it caused only the slightest complication, and was cleared up in a very short time, the news would turn his life around, not just as a talented young hockey player, but as a young man about to discover there was more to life than just hockey.

1954-58

PART TWO

THE FIRST "PRO" CONTRACT

1954-1958

6

THE FORUM IN MONTREAL

ANOTHER SUMMER WAS PASSING, WITH THE USUAL RUN of work, soccer and music occupying much of his time, and still no news of hockey.

It was not until late August that the first contact was made. It came by letter and, surprisingly, not from anyone in the Montreal organization, as expected. It was from Madison Square Gardens, home of the New York Rangers of the NHL. Frank Boucher, the team's general manager, wrote to advise him he had been invited to the Rangers' training camp starting in a few short days in Saskatoon. Phil Watson had been right and perhaps knew that this would be coming all along, but was probably unable to say more than that. George had spent so much time in the Quebec and Montreal hockey environment in the last two years that he had entirely overlooked the Rangers' connection with his contract – they still held his rights as a player. He would even need a refresher as to what the Rangers were doing, who the farm teams were and where the next leg in his hockey quest would probably take him. But there was no way to find out any of that until he got to Saskatchewan for the tryouts.

What he did know was that the tryout with the Rangers would give him the opportunity to sit on the bench with hockey legends Andy Bathgate, Dean Prentice, Bill Gadsby, Nick Mickoski, "Leapin" Lou Fontinato, and defenceman Allan Stanley, together with two of the most famous goaltenders in NHL history: Gump Worsley and Johnny Bower. The thought struck him that all these famous players he had never seen on the ice would now be teammates and friends, game after game – maybe year after year. It was an intimidating prospect.

A day or so after Boucher's letter arrived he received word from an aunt in Grand Falls that she had received an important phone message – "something to do with hockey" – from someone in Montreal, wanting to talk to him. The caller turned out to be Kenny Reardon, assistant general manager of the Montreal Canadiens, and not long retired from their lineup after an eight-year career and five Stanley Cups. It seems Reardon was unaware that George had been signed by the Rangers, and when told that the team had already contacted him with an invitation to their tryouts, he immediately advised him "not to say anything about this call" and that he would be getting back to him. "I'll be in touch" was all he would say further. George was never told what went on after that initial phone call, nor the reason for the call in the first place. All he could do was sit back and wait.

Two days later a telegram arrived at the Canadian National Telegraph Office in Bishop's Falls, with news that would put his life on a course he could never imagine:

> DISREGARD RANGERS TRAINING CAMP. REPORT TO MONTREAL CANADIENS TRAINING CAMP AT MONTREAL FORUM. 9 A.M. SEPTEMBER 9.

After two years of junior hockey and never really knowing whether anything would ever come of it, the moment had finally come for him. It didn't really matter what team it was, as long as it was his long-awaited chance to reach the NHL. Coming as it did – almost overnight – from no less than two NHL teams – made it all the more incredible. The fact that the second call had come from the Canadiens added to the staggering effect he was already feeling from the first news.

It was, too, an extraordinary occasion for the entire Faulkner family, and would not be missed by Lester Faulkner, the wonderful family mentor of all things hockey. But, in such a moment, Lester was lost for words. George's mother, Olive, in typical motherly fashion, thought it might be a good time for celebrating with a big family dinner: the largest moose roast she could dig out of the family freezer. One of her boys, she said, was going to be a *real* hockey player.

"I had been to the Forum a few times before, but now, for the first time I realized how really big it was."

THE FORUM IN MONTREAL

He checked into the Queen's Hotel the night before, after a flight from Gander on an old "bucket of bolts" – a Trans-Canada Airlines *North Star* aircraft – and was joined by a number of other prospects at the camp. Among them was his old friend from Cape Breton, Leo Amadio, and Ray Cyr from New Brunswick. The hotel was owned by Senator Donat Raymond, a hockey icon in Quebec at the time, whose daughter was the wife of Kenny Reardon. It would be their home throughout the three or more weeks of training camp. Next morning, promptly at nine, carrying just his skates, he and the others walked into the Montreal Canadiens dressing room.

The Montreal lineup was fresh off a close Stanley Cup series that spring, finally losing in seven games to their perennial nemesis, the Detroit Red Wings.* The returning lineup was still a formidable one, many of the players still quite young: "The first line was made up of 'Rocket' Richard, Kenny Mosdell and Bert Olmstead. On the second, they had Jean Beliveau, 'Boom Boom' Geoffrion and Dickie Moore." To this day, George laughs as he recites the powerhouse lineup they had that year – the one that he and the other young guys would be trying to break.

In the first few days of camp he played on a line with Donnie Marshall, a swift left winger from Quebec who might be remembered for the slight tuft of hair dominating a receding hairline and boyish face, and lanky Eddie Litzenberger, the 6'3" right winger who would later captain the Chicago Blackhawks to a Stanley Cup win in 1961. They made up the team's fourth line, practising with the team twice a day until the last week or so of camp, when exhibition games took over and they began to play serious hockey with and against the established Montreal players. They knew the final selection would be made up of 20 skaters and 2 goalies, and if they could hang on into the last week of camp, their chances of making it – at least into the farm system – were pretty good. They also knew that Montreal's newest farm team, the Shawinigan Falls Cataracts would be coming

---

* In what has to be the strangest overtime goal in NHL history, Detroit's Tony Leswick flipped the puck high into the Montreal zone to press for a quick line change. Montreal defenceman Doug Harvey tried to intercept the puck with his glove hand and instead deflected it into his own net. The clock showed 4:29 of overtime.

into the Quebec league that year. It would be the team's first year in the league and it came at an opportune time for many of the younger crop of tryouts.

George and the others continued to scan the blackboard for names day after day, as they had in the junior years, and with the exception of a dejected Ray Cyr, the names of Faulkner, Amadio and a young Quebecer who would go on to make the big club later, Junior Langlois, continued to surface.

At the end of week two, the day came when the following blackboard posting appeared:

THE FOLLOWING PLAYERS SHOULD REPORT TO THE SHAWINIGAN FALLS DRESSING ROOM FOR THE NEXT PRACTICE:

The names "Faulkner" and "Amadio" were both on the listing, while Litzenberger's was moved to the Montreal Royals and Marshall's to the AHL's Buffalo Bisons – all now officially professional hockey players for the first time. In George Faulkner's case, it would be an historic moment: he would shortly become the first Newfoundlander ever to sign a professional sports contract.

But before any signing would take place, there was one more significant hurdle to get over: the new players were required to play the first three regular games of the season with Shawinigan before anything became official. It was part of the management's "last look" strategy before signing anyone on the dotted line.* Having played on a line with the likes of "Rocket" Richard and Jean Beliveau, and practicing many one-on-one situations against Montreal's big-five defencemen – certainly the best in the NHL – George didn't consider the further tryout any problem. The morning after he had played the second of the three games, he was called to the office and told they were ready to sign him. They didn't need to see any more. The signing took place in the presence of Kenny Reardon and Shawinigan playing-coach Roger Leger.

"I sat down and signed a contract with Shawinigan for a salary of one hundred and thirty-seven dollars a week. I would've signed for ten."**

---

* Before leaving for Shawinigan they also had to play one exhibition game against the "big team," the Canadiens, losing a close one: 2-1.

** The new players also received a signing bonus of six hundred dollars. In George's case, the entire amount went directly home to his family, together with a new Sunbeam Mixmaster for his mother, Olive.

A moment in his young career equally memorable to the signing that morning happened next day when George and the other hopefuls made their way to the Forum for another day's practice. The group had been using a second dressing room throughout the tryouts, apart from the main area. Even in the traditionally informal atmosphere of training camp there was little to be seen of the senior squad; their dressing room was considered off limits, allowing little social exchange between the two squads. On those days when a planned inter-squad game was about to get underway, the first sighting they'd have of the Montreal players might be when they stepped on the ice for the start of the game, almost as if they'd appeared out of nowhere. On this morning, instead of the usual routine, they were met on their way into the Forum by several team trainers and shown to their new quarters: the main Canadiens' dressing room – hockey's "inner sanctum" at the time.

George walked in, found his own stall, then tentatively surveyed the room. It was the moment of a lifetime, much too real to absorb all at once. Sitting opposite him, dressing quietly, sat Maurice Richard, the famous name and number showing above the stall. "Boom Boom" Geoffrion, a few stalls away, could be heard all over the room – the outgoing, fun-loving character in good form, as usual. Harvey, Johnson, Beliveau – among the best players in the world – surrounded them. In George's mind, there was just this single uneasy thought: "I hope we're not wearing those red team jerseys this morning. I hope it's just the sweats we'll be putting on."

In his sleep that night, images of hockey being played on the Exploits River floated by in a haze of dreams, while one clear image continued to emerge: the likeness of a young boy, maybe ten years old, wearing a New York Rangers sweater.

7

"MIDGE"

SHAWINIGAN, HOME OF OUR TWENTIETH PRIME MINISTER
Jean Chrétien ("the little guy from Shawinigan"), and his wife Aline, and to a
chilling body of water near the falls called Le Trou du Diable (Devil's Hole) for
which its hockey team is named, lies a little more than an hour's drive northeast
of Montreal. It hosts one of the longest established hockey domains in the
province, for many years a notable farm team for the bigger NHL franchises.

The industrial history of the region goes back to its early twentieth- century
hydroelectric potential and development, and later to an expanding aluminum
production facility. Closer to home for the young Faulkner, the area supported
a pulp and paper industry, its way of life and cultural background similar to the
one he knew from childhood. To young athletes seeking a career in hockey, an
additional feature Shawinigan offered was its central location, falling midway
between Montreal and Quebec City, a convenience from many points of view.

His first impression of Shawinigan was its very obvious status as an industrial
town. "Industry was everywhere you looked. Everyone worked. There was no
poverty that you could see. It was a small town, maybe 30,000 people or so,
and always a busy place, always something on the go there." The town stadium
was an old building, looking like it was moving into its last years, with a seating
capacity of less than four thousand. It was filled for every Cataracts game. The
hockey spirit found in cities like Montreal and Quebec City could also be found
in the town of Shawinigan. The fans loved their team and, not unlike those in
every other small Quebec town, wanted a winner every year. In that way, George
remembered, it was always fun to play there, always an enthusiastic, boisterous

crowd coming out each night to support you.

Together with his newfound fortune ("The salary I was getting made me feel like a millionaire"), he teamed up with friends and linemates Connie Broden and Eddie Kachur to find accommodations. The threesome, newly signed professional hockey players – all in their early 20s – rented a small three-bedroom apartment, a first show of independence for all three. Cornell "Connie" Broden and George Faulkner, through their lengthy ties with the Shawinigan Falls organization, would become close friends over the years, and would share somewhat similar destinies within the sport.* Broden was born in Montreal, his brief professional career beginning and ending there. At the time, he was probably one of the few players studying at university while playing in the pro ranks. Kachur, by contrast, spent most of his working life in hockey, a large portion of it in the minor systems.

Hardly before the season began, barely into the first week, Connie Broden suffered a game injury requiring medical attention. The injury was minor, but its occurrence and its consequences, at least for Faulkner, would be profound. During a game against Quebec Aces, Broden received a cut to the head requiring several stitches and necessitating a quick run to the nearest hospital. Nothing serious. When he returned to the apartment, he had a little story to tell: the attending nurse that evening turned out to be a young Newfoundland girl from Bauline. Bertie King had recently moved to Shawinigan with her friend Marjorie Vardy, another Newfoundland nurse who had moved there to join her married sister, Trudy. The Vardy girls hailed from the small West Coast community of Howley, a hub of the forest industry in which nearly all other members of the Vardy family were employed.

In the process of tidying up Connie Broden's forehead, Bertie learned that the young man was a professional hockey player, just settled in Shawinigan, and a close friend and roommate of another Newfoundlander, George Faulkner. "I think the accent gave me away," she laughs, "and brought the topic of New-

---

* Faulkner in 1966, and Broden in 1968, would have outstanding leadership roles with Canada's national team in World Hockey competition.

foundland into the conversation. That's how George's name came up." As well, Trudy Vardy had just returned from a visit to Newfoundland and was told to look up a young man from Bishop's Falls who had recently moved to Shawinigan and was playing hockey there. Trudy had already planned to call George with an invitation to dinner – a small get-together to ease all four Newfoundlanders into their new social and working life in Quebec.

"Can I take my buddy with me?" was how George remembers reacting to the dinner invitation at Trudy Vardy's. "I figured since Connie had already met one of the girls – even though he was lying on a hospital trolley at the time – we'd all feel a bit more comfortable with him along." Broden compared the double invitation to dinner with three women to "something like kissing your grandmother," but joined the group nevertheless. "We'd hardly settled in when all this happened – probably just three or four days since we got to Shawinigan." Broden, a year older than George, was a Montrealer and familiar enough with matters of wining and dining. George, still very much a small-town kid, was anything but comfortable with the whole thing. At this juncture in his new life, the thought of meeting girls from anywhere, let alone from home, was unsettling at best. Nothing in hockey had prepared him for this, and there was nothing in hockey he could compare it to.

The evening turned out to be enjoyable enough. He realized that Marjorie was the one who had made the initial phone call to invite him to dinner, and had met them at the door. She was a petite young brunette and very pretty. He remembered thinking how easy-going she was, how she enjoyed being with people, and how comfortable he was in her presence. On the way home that evening, George and Connie talked about the girls and how everything had gone pretty well, but it was "Midge" (a nickname acquired from her student nursing days in St. John's) who got most of the attention.

"So, whad'ya think of Midge?" said Broden. "You were looking at her all night." Broden knew there was something in the air.

In what must be the all-time most casual, most unromantic comeback, George could only manage to say, "She looked pretty good to me."

Less than a week later, they were sitting in a movie theater, their first time together in what would become a lifelong relationship.

8

THE QUEBEC HOCKEY LEAGUE

The first thing you learn after becoming a pro is that this is a serious business and you have to produce. The fun of the game takes on a new perspective. But the thrill of the game never changes. You're still just a kid out there.

THE QUEBEC HOCKEY LEAGUE (QHL) GREW OUT OF THE old Quebec Senior Hockey League (QSHL), which disbanded rather dramatically after the 1952-53 season.* The new league moved from amateur to semi-professional status, and in its first season, 1954-55, operated with six teams: Shawinigan Falls Cataracts, Quebec Aces, Montreal Royals, Chicoutimi Sagueneens, Valleyfield Braves and Ottawa Senators. The league was highly competitive, hosting a multitude of professional players on the fringe of NHL careers, and continued the long-established success of its predecessor of a year ago. Attendance, with one exception, was beyond expectations. The Ottawa Senators fell short in fan support and were forced to withdraw from competition in late December. The new league and the town of Shawinigan Falls would be home to George Faulkner for the next four years.

---

* The league was formed out of frustration with Jean Beliveau's refusal to sign with the Montreal Canadiens, preferring to stay with the Quebec Aces, an amateur club at the time. By purchasing the entire league and designating it as 'semi-professional', Montreal's Frank Selke was able to force the issue with Beliveau and finally sign him to a professional contract.

The last three years of his life, from his leaving home at age 17 to when he signed on with the Cataracts, now seemed like forever. The entire hockey experience – the travel, the games, the practice schedules, the threatening coaches, the absence of home – all seemed to suddenly come together in his mind as a single moment from a long time ago. The fact that he had made it this far reinforced the thought that he could make the big leagues. He had always been able to measure his own abilities against the competition at each level he played, and he was able to do so now. He knew he could compete. Like so much else in life, all he needed now was a break.

In many respects the year ahead would be the most successful and satisfying in his short career. His linemates – Broden and Kachur – were also his closest friends, and equally bent on making it to the NHL – a "three musketeers" kind of friendship developing as they began their careers in Shawinigan. Each would perform better than ever, contributing in a big way to the team's success during the year. The Cataracts would dominate the league in regular-season play, and would once again challenge for the league championship and a shot at Canada's top prize in this new league – the Edinburgh Trophy. Not that the other teams in the division were any kind of pushovers. The competition was challenging at every turn, the rivalries serious and aggressive. But the Cataracts somehow gelled as a unit that year: there were few injuries, no in-fighting, no quarrels to upset the rhythm of games night after night.

Even the league's travel arrangements were comfortable. The travel by team bus from Shawinigan was no more than an hour or so from each venue, with the exception of games scheduled with the Chicoutimi squad, which took them past Montreal and into the Laurentians for a lengthy three-hour run.

Apart from "the three musketeers," the team carried other promising NHLers, among them defencemen Jean-Guy Talbot and Bob Turner, and right winger Claude Provost. Provost, a Montreal native, was called up to Shawinigan Falls that year after spending three years with the Junior Canadiens and often played on a line with Broden and Faulkner. The threesome would excel in playmaking and scoring during the year and into the playoffs. At the same time, another bright Canadiens prospect, Henri Richard, was beginning his last year with the Junior Canadiens in Montreal. All four were within a year of joining the senior Habs. Their individual career successes would be determined, as always, by personal injuries, differing needs within the make-up of the

Canadiens team, and the indisputable assessments of its coach, Toe Blake. As the season began for the Cataracts, it seemed the stars were aligned favourably for the team, its "three musketeers," and its immediate future.

The Shawinigan Falls Cataracts would have a rather disappointing start to the 1954-55 season, losing their first game of the year to Valleyfield but then quickly begining a run of seven straight wins. By the end of October, they found themselves in first place in the league. George's play was consistently strong, and apart from a slight knee injury which kept him out of the lineup for a few games early in the season, he played regular shifts at left wing – often playing 30 minutes a game – and took turns on the team's power play, along with Broden and Talbot.

As the season progressed, George felt more and more comfortable with his role with the Cataracts, and his play continued to improve considerably. His social life slowly began to follow the same pattern, as the relationship between himself and Midge continued to grow. "Shawinigan's social structure was pretty simple. There was not always a lot to see or do, so we spent most of the time at her place along with Bertie and Midge's sister Trudy. I bought an old Gibson guitar at the time – I still have it – and tried my hand at entertaining whenever I visited. That's how bad things were."

Within a few weeks of their meeting, Midge informed him that she and Bertie had applied for positions as stewardesses with Trans-Canada Airlines (TCA) and were expected to join the airline after Christmas, although no official word had yet been received. To qualify back then, a stewardess had to be single and possess a nursing licence – "certified and single," as the expression was in the early days of flying. As things turned out, both received word to be in Montreal in early January to begin their six-week training course, and then be ready to immediately criss-cross the country in their new roles. As George would soon find out, the only hitch in their plans was lack of funding to rent an apartment in Montreal. They had only started work in Shawinigan that summer and just as quickly decided to apply for a higher-paying, and certainly a more exciting, work experience in this new profession. They managed to save very little in the meantime. "I remember I got a call from Midge a day or so after they arrived in Montreal. She was pretty embarrassed to have to ask for a loan, since we had barely just met, but they were desperate and needed $150 dollars to get them started. I just laughed at her predicament and sent the money off right away. It was pretty obvious how I felt about her at the time."

The Cataracts steamrolled through the regular schedule. Near the end of March their record stood at 39 wins in 62 games, some 13 points ahead of second-place Quebec Aces and its bad-tempered, often aggressive team manager that year, George "Punch" Imlach. Imlach had played for the Aces a decade before, during a four-year stretch beginning in 1945, a short-lived and non-descript playing career, before moving into the coaching ranks. In four years' time he would finally reach the NHL as coach of the Toronto Maple Leafs. Before reaching the big time, he would have to experience several disappointments in his coaching debut, beginning with the 1955 playoffs in the Quebec league. His young Quebec Aces finished the season in second place, well behind the Cataracts, and then lost the semi-finals to the third-place Montreal Royals. Meanwhile, the Cataracts would defeat the fourth-place Chicoutimi Sangueens, losing only two games in that series.

The league finals, a best-of-seven affair, would be George's first playoffs in the professional leagues and would be played as a home-and-home match-up at the Forum in Montreal and the Shawinigan-Falls Arena. The games at the Forum would be played before crowds of twelve thousand – intimidating enough for a kid from the Exploits River.

The first game was played at the Forum on a Sunday afternoon with a relatively small crowd of six thousand onlookers. The Cataracts lost, 4-3, with Broden and Kachur contributing to the scoring while George was held without a point. Game two, played on an auspicious day in world news,* would be a different affair: the team would win at home, 4-2, with Faulkner getting one goal and one assist before a full house of some six thousand.

The series was now tied at one game each. The Royals' coaching staff, realizing they needed more strength up front, decided to call up a promising young player, Phil Goyette, from the International League's Cincinnati Mohawks. His presence made no impression on the Cataracts, however. They

63

---

* The success of the Salk vaccine experiments in the fight against polio, the epidemic, crippling childhood disease, was announced publicly on April 12, 1955.

went on to win once again at home, with goalie Bob Perreault getting his first playoff shutout, 4-0, before 5,300 fans in Shawinigan.

In game four, however, played at the Forum, they were outplayed handily, losing by a score of 5-1, a one-sided trimming that did not go unnoticed by the fans back home in Shawinigan. The series was again deadlocked, but the Cataracts could at least look forward to game five at home to give them some much needed momentum. Instead, things seemed to get worse. At the end of the second period in game five, they found themselves down by two goals to the Royals. The score stood at 3-1. A loss at home in this one, and they faced an almost certain elimination in the next game back in Montreal.

Another five thousand fans crowded the arena that night, and, as the Cataracts took to the ice for the start of the third period, the Shawinigan fans – in a totally unusual gesture – stood and booed their home team in frustration. The message was clear and it got through to George Faulkner and his teammates in a hurry. Faulkner became an instant hero with five minutes left in the period when he tied the game, assisted by Connie Broden, his biggest moment in professional hockey so far. He thought the arena would come apart. A few moments later Eddie Kachur completed the team's exciting comeback with an unassisted winner late in the game.

The next game – game six – would prove to be the last in that series, with Shawinigan winning easily, 4-1. Faulkner and Broden drew one point each in that finale. In total points scored in the series, four rookies would lead the way: Connie Broden at 12 points (6 goals, 6 assists); George Faulkner at 5-5, and Claude Provost in his first season with Shawinigan, at 6-3. Eddie Kachur finished with 7 points.

The series against the Montreal Royals finished up on April 21. The team would have only one day's rest before the start of the best-of-nine finals for the Canadian championship against the Edmonton Flyers, representing the West. It was East meets West for the newly minted Edinburgh Trophy. To offset transportation costs, the entire series would be played in the East,* a home-and-

---

* Cross-Canada flights were not yet commonplace in the country, and travel time from east to west by rail would not be practical. The start of the series was also delayed until the Stanley Cup finals were completed, allowing for more TV and media exposure for the new league.

home affair at Shawinigan and Montreal. Despite a long and now waning year of hockey, attendance would continue to be steady, and the series itself would be exciting, featuring no less than three overtime games.

One look at the Edmonton Flyers lineup would explain why the series would produce good hockey and be more than competitive for the Cataracts. Norman "Bud" Poile, former Toronto Maple Leaf player from the 1940s and now Edmonton's playing-coach, headed the list, followed by Edmonton's leading scorers – Bronco Horvath, Johnny Bucyk and Norm Ullman. Other future NHL stalwarts included Vic Stasiuk, Al Arbour, Gerry Melnyk and Hall of Fame goalie, Glenn Hall. Coming into the series, Horvath, Bucyk and Ullman had combined point totals for the regular season at 105 goals and 152 assists. But the play of Glenn Hall would prove to be even more threatening.

Game one was scheduled for Saturday, April 23, in Shawinigan Falls. Glenn Hall's amazing and often acrobatic talents were already creating a stir in hockey circles that year. It was obvious he was destined for the NHL – and very soon – and that he would become one of the greatest goalies of all time, ironically replacing Detroit's Terry Sawchuk, who is, in the opinion of many, perhaps *the* greatest goalie of all time. The move by Detroit would come at the end of the 1955 season when Sawchuk was traded to Boston in a seven-player deal.

Shawinigan, in a rather surprising outcome to many, claimed the 1955 Edinburgh Trophy, winning the series five games to two. With one exception, Shawinigan outshot the Flyers in every game of that series, a seven-game shootout featuring three overtime games, a goal differential of only 25-19, and another impressive scoring and point display by Shawinigan's rookie line of Faulkner, Broden and Kachur. The threesome, along with newcomer Claude Provost, who sometimes shared double-duty as their linemate during the series, collected 21 points in the seven games played.

No sooner had the season ended and George had made his way back home, when he learned that Midge had applied to work the airline's eastern Canada route, switching from flights out west to Winnipeg and beyond. Unlike today's world of high-speed jet travel favouring heavily populated areas, while so-called "regional" airlines service the smaller centres, air travel in the 1950s took in both large and small towns and cities. A late-night flight from Montreal to St. John's, for example, would be an all-night journey, stopping at Fredericton, Moncton, Halifax, Sydney, Stephenville and Gander before the final leg into St. John's, some eight to ten hours later. "Frequent fliers" back then could log more take-offs and landings in a year than some jet pilots do today.

In her newly assigned regional flying role, Midge made regularly scheduled stops in Gander, usually a mere fifteen-minute stopover. She still maintained her apartment in Montreal with Bertie and a couple of other TCA stewardesses. George would drive the 60 miles of dirt road from Bishop's Falls to Gander, make a crossing on the Exploits River via Joe Hampton's ferry (affectionately called "the scow") just to see her. On one of her first stopovers that summer, George decided to have his father and his younger sister, Marie, tag along with him on the run to Gander to meet the "new woman" in his life. It seems Lester Faulkner, a railway engineer, was more than familiar with Midge's hometown of Howley, having passed through the community on his many railway runs to Newfoundland's west coast. "Dad used to pass by their house on his frequent runs into Howley. Even watched them wave from their front steps sometimes." The meeting was an easy one. Seems Lester knew more of the circumstances about life in Howley than anyone had realized before that first meeting.

Except for those brief stopovers at Gander, Midge and George spent no time together all that summer. Such were the vagaries of romance and flying schedules back then.

9

THE SOPHOMORE YEAR

THE 1955-56 QHL SEASON, HIS SECOND AS A PRO, WOULD see George get off to his best start ever, scoring six goal in six games. He was well ahead of last season's pace. Coincidentally, at some point early in the season, he learned from coach Roger Leger that his name was on the "call-up" list for the senior club, reflecting his status with the organization as certainly well recognized. It would not be long, however, before a series of events would turn his good fortune, at least for the moment, in another direction. It began with his second knee injury early in October, which sidelined him for 12 games, slowing the momentum of the great start to the year he was enjoying. Meanwhile, in the very first game of the season, Canadiens' right winger and star forward Bernie "Boom Boom" Geoffrion took a bad spill coming from behind his net, injuring his back and forcing him out of the lineup for 11 games. The injury uprooted him temporarily from linemates Jean Beliveau and Dickie Moore, probably the highest-scoring trio in the game that year. Everyone on the Shawinigan Cataracts knew the call-up would come from one of their number, and it turned out, logically in this case, to be another up-and-coming right-handed shooter, Claude Provost.*

Provost, who had proven his worth in his first season with the team, with 25 goals and 48 points, was just nine games into the QHL season when the call

---

* Provost may best be remembered for his famous "shadow" assignment on Chicago's Bobby Hull in the 1961 Stanley Cup playoffs with the Blackhawks. Hull could do little against the irritating Provost, but Chicago managed to win that semi-final series and go on to win the Stanley Cup that year.

came. Best known as a defensive-style forward with a somewhat awkward skating style, he would fit nicely into coach Toe Blake's defensive strategies for the team, but it was a far cry from the scoring punch which Geoffrion could give them. In the first few weeks with the Canadiens, Provost saw little ice time. Blake used him occasionally to "shake up" the Canadien game style with his spirited, aggressive play. On one occasion, the team lost two games in a row – a considerable setback by Montreal standards – and it was Provost's job to get them moving again. Whatever need he filled for the club at the time, it seemed to work: the team was soon back in winning form. One way or another, it looked from the outset that he was with the Canadiens to stay. In fact, Claude Provost would spend the rest of his career with the Montreal Canadiens, a member of its five consecutive Stanley Cup winning teams from 1956 to 1960, the so-called dynasty, along with rookies Henri Richard, Bob Turner and Jean-Guy Talbot. However, only Provost and Richard would spend their entire careers with the Canadiens organization.

As George Faulkner watched the names on the "call-up" list come and go that year, there was one point when it seemed his time had finally come. Dickie Moore received a slight shoulder injury, and, as George himself tells it, the need for a strong left-winger on the senior club arose, if only for a short while: "I was a left-handed shot, like Dickie, who often played on a line with Beliveau at centre and Maurice Richard on right-wing.* When Dickie got hurt, I thought I might get the call but instead they switched Provost, an established right winger all his life, to the left side." Even teammate Gilles Dube, a left-hander who was leading the team in scoring that year, was overlooked by Blake and his coaching staff in favour of Provost. The incident must have left a heavy mark on the psyche and morale of both players.

The Saturday, October 29, 1955, edition of the *Montreal Gazette* featured two new hockey items on its sports page that day – both in headline format. The first showed pictures of Cataracts' goalie Bob Perreault, a Trois-Rivières native, who had allowed only nine goals in eleven games so far that young season, and a youngster from Newfoundland, 21-year-old George Faulkner, who was having his best start yet with six goals in as many games. The item was run by *The Gazette*

---

* The "Rocket" was a left-handed shot who played right-wing his entire career.

to give some clout to the upcoming match between first-place Shawinigan Falls Cataracts and the home team – second-place Montreal Royals. The game would also be televised in one of the first Sunday afternoon telecasts in Quebec at the time.

The same page carried headlines and a story of how a young Claude Provost had been called up recently to put some drive into the team after the Canadiens lost two straight games, which coach Toe Blake, in typical Blake fashion, considered nothing short of humiliation. Geoffrion was scheduled to return the following day for a game against the Leafs, but Blake wasn't sure whether the injured Geoffrion was quite ready to come back so soon to play a full game. Provost, according to Blake's plan, would fill in for Geoffrion if needed. It happened that he continued to play left-wing for most of the game, the envied position of all left-handed shooters on the Shawinigan club.

Meanwhile, the much-touted Sunday televised game between the Royals and Cataracts had the Shawinigan lads lose the moment and the game, 5-2. George managed to get a spot on camera in that game, drawing one assist in the team's failing effort. In the Canadiens' game, Provost did the same: getting one assist in Sunday's 2-2 tie with Detroit. Not a bad weekend for both young players.

In many ways, the second Cataracts season seemed to duplicate the pattern of the previous year. The team was leading the league and seemingly well on its way to another Canadian championship. Even team statistics for the year would show much similarity with the year before. Eddie Kachur would have his best year so far, leading the "musketeers" in scoring with 31 goals, his best output ever. Connie Broden was not far behind, followed by Faulkner, who would miss 12 games before the Christmas break with another bothersome knee injury. The loss of so many games after his exciting early start to the season probably deprived George of his first 25-goal year in the professional ranks.

Nearly two-thirds into the season, the Shawinigan Falls Cataracts were holding fast to their lead over the Montreal Royals. In early January, Montreal's "Pocket Rocket" Richard was injured, along with star defenceman Doug Harvey with a hand injury. Claude Provost and Jean-Guy Talbot had already been called up to the senior club and would not return – their careers firmly in the hands of the senior club. Now it became the turn of "little" Connie Broden and the Cataracts' most outstanding defenceman, Bob Turner. For Broden, the call-up would be temporary, a mere three-game trial. For Turner, it would be the final step in an up-and-coming career in the big leagues. He wasted no time in his role as fill-in for Harvey, impressing the Montreal organization with the same forceful style of play that was his trademark in Shawinigan.

The league standings at this point had Shawinigan with 24 wins and 50 points, ten points ahead of the Royals, while individual league scoring statistics had George and his linemates in the thick of things. Despite games missed earlier on, George's output continued to be strong, with 13 goals and 10 assists. In the goaltending department, veteran Bob Perreault held third place behind leader Gerry McNeil of the Royals and Marcel Paille of Chicoutimi, both destined for lengthy NHL careers.

On the night of February 7, 1956, Detroit's Gordie Howe scored his 300th and 301st career goals against the lowly Chicago Blackhawks, tying Jean Beliveau for the league scoring lead with 60 points each after 52 games. Meanwhile, in Shawinigan, George Faulkner and Connie Broden were stretching the team's first place lead to 13 points over the Montreal Royals, killing any hope the Royals might have had of catching them. Shawinigan defeated Quebec Aces that night 2-1, with Faulkner scoring the team's first goal, assisted by Broden. There were just 17 games left in the season.

The Shawinigan Cataracts would go on to finish in first place that year, easily outpointing the ever-dangerous Montreal Royals for the second-straight season. But the Royals would have their revenge in the 1956 round of playoffs, a series that, as the expression goes, "had everything." The Cataracts fell to the Royals in game six of the finals on April 21, a Sunday afternoon game that would be remembered by both George and Midge for a couple of reasons. Midge was working a full schedule during that time, and she knew that this game had the Cataracts on the brink of elimination. On the return flight home to Montreal that day, she couldn't wait for the scheduled stopover in Sydney to check the final score with a local radio station. "Did they win or lose?" she asked, only to learn that they had lost 2-1 at the Forum in the third overtime.

Despite the disappointment, the news did not cause a great deal of upset. That afternoon she had more important things on her mind than the outcome of a hockey game. She had a wedding to get ready for, and only a week in which to do it. Their wedding – all planned for many weeks now – was only a few days away: Saturday, April 28, in Shawinigan. On her arrival in Montreal that evening, the first thing she did was pass in her resignation with the airline. In a week's time, she would no longer qualify under the "certified and single" regulation.

For 22-year-old George Faulkner, losing that series would mark the end of a long string of consecutive winning seasons, going back to his first year of Junior "B" with the Quebec Citadelles, a total of eight in all. He finished the year in good standing, despite the loss of games through injury, with a record of 17 goals and 33 points. In many ways, however, it was the end of a disappointing season: a great start, followed by a sudden injury, and no call-up in his second professional year, while at the same time five of his teammates – Talbot, Turner, Provost, Broden and Perreault – had seen action in the NHL. Nevertheless, he continued to believe that maybe the next year would bring about a change in that circumstance.

For now, like his fiancé, Midge Vardy, he too had other things on his mind. The timing couldn't be better.

The wedding was a small, subdued affair. There was no one from home on either side of the families. Several of Midge's friends from the airline made it to the ceremony and reception ("a little get-together"), which was held in sister Trudy's home. The one Newfoundland element was the minister who performed the ceremony, a Reverend Belbin, stationed in Quebec at the time. "I remember we had a single bottle of something called "Harvey's Shooting Sherry." That was all we had to drink, because none of us drank anyway. I don't know if we even opened it." For all anyone knows, it might still be there.

They honeymooned for two weeks in Florida, thanks to Midge's connections with Trans-Canada Airlines. George remembers stepping off the plane that first day wearing the same heavy blue serge wedding suit with a red carnation still attached, the heat of a late April day almost stifling him as he made his way to the terminal. The change from the cold Quebec air and the constant chill of hockey arenas was striking, but more than welcome. They had two full weeks of celebration and relaxation ahead of them, the first of many trips to the South together. The honeymoon was perfect.

They returned home to a Newfoundland spring almost as warm and inviting as Florida had been, their living accommodations for the rest of that year a matter of alternating trips between Bishop's Falls and Howley the entire time. The train ride each way, from Deer Lake to Howley – there were no roads into Howley as yet – would often have them in the company of Lester Faulkner, who'd be up front running things in the engineer's compartment. There was no work to be done that summer, nothing but lounging and relaxing, until the call came once again from Montreal in late August – another year in the wilds of Shawinigan's hockey world, but this time together.

The end of his second professional hockey season (1955-56) saw George Faulkner's career destiny tighten more than ever under the control of the Montreal Canadiens. The team that year launched the first of five of the most successful seasons ever recorded, with perhaps the strongest lineups the game had ever seen. The record, five straight Stanley Cups, 1956-60, remains intact today, and, in the opinion of many, will never be broken. The closest anyone has ever come to equaling that record was the same Montreal Canadiens (1976-79), and the New York Islanders (1980-83).

Any discussion of the Montreal dynasty of those record years always turns on a point of who was most responsible for such an accomplishment, and it usually begins with the name, Hector "Toe" Blake.

The guys who played under him always paint Toe Blake as fair but demanding, tough and exacting, a man who hated to lose. He would never berate a player in public, even in front of his teammates, ever aware that a player's personal dignity went beyond the game of hockey. Whenever it became necessary to take someone to task, he'd always find a place somewhere private before "letting him have it." There was also the side of him, a very wise side, which allowed the players to play their own game, no matter what crisis or catastrophe faced the team. "Play the way that got you here" was one of his favourite admonitions to younger players. Perhaps the well-known Montreal sports columnist Red Fisher, describing the man he knew so well during these years, sums up Toe Blake most succinctly: "If there was one dominant figure on the team that won five straight Stanley Cups, I think it would have to be Toe Blake. This guy was a kindly old coach, a gentleman, and a son of a bitch, all in the same sentence."

Many of Blake's players liked to recall the emphasis he placed on "strategy," not in the sense of a game-by-game or opponent-by-opponent pattern, but in a consistent belief that his team's success was built primarily on defence, coupled with a consistently strong offence, which was understood to come through game after game. Some say he built the club around the scoring prowess of just two offensive forward lines, with a third line pegged primarily as a defensive unit. Combine that strategy with four or five of the most accomplished defencemen in the league – one of whom was the great Doug Harvey, whose offensive skills often surpassed his defensive abilities – and you win the Stanley Cup – five years running.

No team in hockey has ever gone anywhere without good goaltending – a point of the game proven time and again, and still very true today. Weak goaltending – especially at playoff time – was the perennial Achilles' heel of great teams over the years, and no amount of offence could offset that reality. Jacques Plante proved to be that necessary component during the great Montreal years, just as Terry Sawchuk, Glenn Hall and Ken Dryden performed their own miracles when the time came to win.

On the other side of all that talent, the question must be asked: what were the chances of promising younger players in the Montreal system* ever breaking into such a lineup? Such was the reality facing many of the Shawinigan Cataracts hopefuls, including, and very near the top of that list, George Faulkner. He had just completed his best year and had shown a consistency in his game that would continue for the next two years, until the end of the 1958 season. He had been invited to four Montreal Canadiens training camps in each of the four years with Shawinigan and remained on their NHL call-up list on a regular basis. Nevertheless, it was apparent that few lineup changes would happen while the Canadiens continued to win. And, as the record shows, new faces breaking into that lineup were few, and mostly defensive in the style of game they played.

Ironically, Blake's shadow was all over the success of the Montreal Canadiens as much as it diminished the chances of young talents waiting in line to join them.

---

* Montreal had farm teams in Buffalo and Cincinnati, the Royals in Montreal and Shawinigan, to name a few.

10

A NEW START

*No one could ever figure out what happened to us that year.
We went from first place to fifth, almost overnight, and yet there were no
big changes in the team, no obvious reasons to explain what happened.
We knew we had to really try to shake things up the next year.*

THE 1956-57 SEASON WAS INDEED A STRANGE ONE.
The Cataracts had lost the league championship in a tense, seventh-game
overtime just a few months before, and when the new season began it was as if
they could hardly tie their own skates. The team that had won 43 games the
year before, losing only 18, suddenly fell 34 points below last year's standings,
and 32 points behind first-place Quebec Aces. Yet the team roster had shown
little significant change. Turner and Provost were both gone, but replaced
by Junior Langlois and Andre Pronovost, both top NHL prospects. Veteran
goalie Bob Perreault, always a steadying factor for the team, was joined that year
by back-up goalie Charlie Hodge, a youthful 23-year-old and future Montreal
Canadien. Goaltending would certainly not be one of the team's problems. No
one could explain the collapse.

The Ottawa Junior Canadiens ("Les Baby Habs"), playing across the river
in Hull, Quebec, joined the league for a 20-game schedule that year, in an
unusual set-up that allowed them to compete/exhibit in two other leagues as
well. The Montreal organization was looking for the best competition they
could find for the younger players, and in the process saved the Cataracts from

finishing last, at least on paper. Nevertheless, the season was a dismal one. The team played through most of the first month of the season with an 0-5 record, including two home-ice shutouts. Finally, on October 29, they came alive with a 5-0 trouncing of the Quebec Aces, and ended the month with a victory at the Forum, 5-2 against the Royals, the only two wins that month against seven losses.

George's play was little help during the first half of the season. In fact, the Broden-Faulkner-Kachur threesome was somewhat tame throughout the early part of that season: a goal here and there, and the odd assist to at least keep their names on the score sheet. Many of the teams' losses were by one-goal deficits, low-scoring affairs which offered little opportunity for anyone on the team to get on the score sheet very often.

It didn't help players' morale when a first-game injury to Montreal's Henri Richard on October 13 resulted in a call-up to the senior club of Ralph Backstrom, a promising member of the Junior Canadiens, for a three-game trial. When a flu bug hit the Montreal team that same week and both "Boom Boom" Geoffrion and Floyd Curry had to sit out weekend games in New York, their replacements were Guy Rousseau of the Montreal Royals and Gerry Wilson,* also of the Junior Canadiens. Team members of the suddenly struggling Shawinigan Cataracts watched as yet another opportunity passed them by that year, and they had to be affected by it.

Seeming to add insult to injury, the last game of November, played on the 30th, had them lose in yet another poor display, 5-2, to the "Baby Habs," the league's traveling sideshow that season. Revenge for this one would not come until near season's end, when George and company walloped the Canadiens from Hull, 12-3, in what would be the most lopsided score in the league that year. However, nothing changed in the standings as a result.

Shawinigan ended the season as it had begun, playing with an unfamiliar inconsistency for the first time. Luckily, it would not be repeated. They finished in fifth and last place, 30 points behind first place Quebec Aces, and missed league playoffs for the first time in their brief history.

---

* In later years, Gerry, also known as Jerry, became team doctor of the Winnipeg Jets, Winnipeg Blue Bombers and the Royal Winnipeg Ballet. Suffering lifelong knee problems, he managed only three career games in the NHL, all with Montreal.

Eddie Kachur, the tough little right-winger with the "three musketeers" line, played only 32 games for Shawinigan before moving up at last to the NHL for a 34-game set with last-place Chicago Blackhawks, the first of the "musketeers" to move on. The opening for Kachur brought back memories of a little-known decision made by the Canadiens' organization back in 1954-55, which had to do with Broden's and Faulkner's first opportunity to play in the big time.

At the end of that season, 1954-55, Montreal coach Dick Irvin Sr., decided to leave Monreal – after 15 consecutive years behind the bench – to try and salvage what he could of perennial last-place finishers Chicago Blackhawks. Irvin saw potential in Broden and Faulkner from the outset and made a bid to have them play in Chicago, along with young Claude Provost. Ironically, Kachur, the first of the three to actually make it to the NHL, was not included in the deal. Irvin was confident that Provost, Broden and Faulkner would put new life into the desperate Blackhawks' lineup. The move looked to be a good one, and the timing coincided nicely with his new position in Chicago. However, the Montreal organization refused the offer. It seems any chance to get new blood into the NHL with other teams was not a consideration for the Montreal organization. They would keep what they had, unless it meant trading up.

With the loss of Eddie Kachur, George Faulkner felt the breakup of the "musketeer" connection deeply. Looking back at Dick Irvin's gesture at the time, he would always wonder what might have become of the three of them in Chicago Blackhawk uniforms.*

No doubt Kachur's absence had anything but a positive effect on Connie Broden as well. It would prove to be their last season together. Kachur stayed with the Blackhawks throughout the rest of the 1956-57 season before moving back to Buffalo in the AHL in 1958. Meanwhile, Connie Broden, no doubt looking carefully ahead at his own future in hockey, played out the full schedule of 68 games with the Cataracts, showing totals of 20 goals and 29 assists for fourth place in the team's scoring. It would prove to be his last year with the club.

---

* Dick Irvin's Blackhawks finished last again that year. He was expected to stay with the club for the next season, 1955-56, but took seriously ill before the season began. Irvin died from bone cancer on May 15, 1957.

George, despite the uncertainties surrounding the game that year and missing 13 games, managed to end the year once again with a spirited 19 goals and 26 assists for a sixth-place finish in the team's point standings. All in all, the season had not been a complete disaster, despite the team's poor performance.

He was soon to discover that maybe the best of the 1956-57 hockey year, though now officially completed, was yet to come.

The ill wind of his first losing season soon swung about, bringing him an interesting venture at season's end. As part of an ongoing hockey tradition of that era, members of teams failing to make the playoffs were often invited by Gerry Regan, a Halifax lawyer,* to join a handsomely paying exhibition tour of the Maritimes, including several stops and exhibition games across Newfoundland. The pay was twenty-five dollars per game, all expenses paid, and the very best of accommodations everywhere they went. Regan made the tour an annual Maritime event, and the 1957 version would turn out to be an especially memorable affair for the young Newfoundland native. The collection of players joining the tour – most of them members of the Shawinigan team, with a few "make-up" junior league players, including three from the Junior Canadiens – travelled by car to scheduled games throughout New Brunswick and Nova Scotia before crossing the Gulf to play before eager and excited Newfoundland fans. This particular exhibition series would have them play 13 games in 14 nights, in front of sold-out crowds from start to finish. The final games of the tour would be played at the recently opened St. John's Memorial Stadium, with double-headers and opposing all-star teams before as many as three thousand spectators. Another anticipated venue, and perhaps highlight of the tour for George, was his old home base – the Grand Falls Stadium.

The homefolks in Bishop's and Grand Falls had planned a big surprise for him, an unexpected change of plans from all the other games. The homecoming contest would have all five Faulkners – Lindy, George, Alex, Seth and Jack – in uniform for the Grand Falls team against the visiting mainlanders. Two of the five brothers, Alex and Jack, would soon join their older brother in the professional hockey ranks. The strength of the Faulkners would maybe even up

---

* Gerald Regan later became premier of Nova Scotia.

the odds against the visiting pros. It would certainly cause quite a stir with their hometown fans in Bishop's Falls.

At the same time, the two weeks away from home would give Midge a chance to spend time visiting a sister in New York, allowing George all the freedom in the world to play the game in a different mindset for a change. The players knew from the start that the competition throughout the tour was really no match for them, so they could lay back and have fun during each game – scoring at will, or slowing it down, allowing a few goals now and then to make sure the hometown fans had something to cheer about. Terry Sawchuk, playing with the Boston Bruins during a similar tour in 1956, often just stood in his goal crease reading a newspaper during the game. Either way, the emphasis was on entertainment and fun – most of the time. On the Newfoundland segment of the tour, things would get somewhat unpleasant in Gander, thanks to a scuffle and some roughhouse play involving Reggie Fleming, a newcomer to Shawinigan, and a born "enforcer." In later years, this same behaviour established him as one of hockey's "bad boys" for most of his NHL career.

The tour was scheduled for the first week of April, beginning in Corner Brook with a two-game exhibition stop. The best of the Corner Brook senior league players were selected to carry the town's colors, most of them seeing professional hockey players for the first time, and, unfortunately, living to regret it. The Quebec team outscored Corner Brook 22-10, despite their obvious attempt not to embarrass. In the last few minutes of the game, the contest looked more like entertainment – with all kinds of frolicking taking the place of a serious hockey game. Despite the score, the fans loved every minute. Like the members of their team, it was the spectators' first experience seeing the skills of the game displayed at that level, and it was a real eye-opener.

In Grand Falls only a day later, the team prepared for perhaps its biggest competition of the tour, the Grand Falls Bees, who had just won the All-Newfoundland championship and would include in its lineup all four of the remaining Faulkner clan: Lindy, Alex, Seth and 14-year-old Jack. The local newspaper, the Grand Falls *Advertiser*, carried an item about the touring Quebec team and suggested to its organizers that George should play with the Grand Falls squad; in fact, that all five Faulkners play on the same shifts for that game. The idea took hold, and it wasn't long before the whole town was buzzing about the prospect of five of their own taking to the ice against all those professionals.

The game itself was everything they expected. In the first period, a disappointed 2,400 fans watched their heroes fall behind 6-0. Despite being outplayed most of the time, the local press coverage had them hitting the post no less than seven times. At the end of the second period, it stood at 10-4 for the Quebecers. As expected, the roof nearly came off the Grand Falls Stadium at the start of the third period when all five Faulkners, wearing the Grand Falls team uniform, took to the ice for the drop of the puck. George recalls wearing a pair of hockey pants for that game that "were four sizes too big and held up with marlin twine instead of braces." There was no doubting where the fans' allegiance lay from that point on. The final score turned out to be 11-9 for the visitors, but in that third-period exchange between teams, the Faulkners managed to accumulate six points: George, with one goal and three assists, and Alex and young Jack Faulkner with one goal each. George remembers in the dressing room, at the end of the game, how teammate Reggie Fleming commented on Alex Faulkner's abilities: "That kid could easily be playing with us." Alex was only 20 at the time, and still three years away from a professional start, but acknowledged even then as probably the best hockey player in Newfoundland.

After finishing with two teams from central Newfoundland, the Quebecers were now ready for teams representing Bell Island and St. John's. A game with a hastily arranged group of Newfoundland All-stars would round out the tour. Getting into St. John's proved to be a problem. The roads were impassable at the time, the train schedule was temporarily shut down,* and there were no commercial aircraft available to fly them from Gander. Not to be outdone, Gerry Regan had a quick solution: the team would fly to St. John's compliments of a Newfoundland water-bomber. "We piled our gear into the belly of the water bomber

---

* Newfoundland's West Coast experienced a violent winter storm during the first week of April 1957, at the site of the infamous Gaff Topsails, burying two of the railway's express trains with 137 passengers on board.

and then jumped in and used the bags to lie or sit on." A windy, bumpy ride into St. John's had them less than ready to play hockey. No time for meals or warm-ups for this game, "not even a cup of hot tea." Instead, they arrived late, still feeling the effects of a very cold and disorienting plane ride.

Adding to their misfortune, in just a few short minutes they would be facing perhaps the most rugged team on the island – the Bell Island Islanders, a talented and determined squad like no other. The final outcome was 12-7 for Regan's professionals, but goalie Fraser-Betts Shaw, a last-minute replacement from Cape Breton, had his busiest night by far. Bell Island's Martin Craig and Neil Kennedy had two goals each, while Joe Byrne, Bill Power and Gordie Skanes had one each. Typically, the Bell Islanders wanted no part of entertainment during the game: they meant business from start to finish, impressing the Quebec professionals in every period played.

As he did after each game played, Gerry Regan appeared in the Quebecers' dressing room after the game that night – a little edgier than usual because of the strong performance put on by the Bell Islanders – and distributed the team's pay – in one-dollar bills – to each player. No waiting for lengthy paydays on this tour. "He'd simply drop the 25 bills, one by one, in front of each player as he moved around the dressing room, laughing all the while." Just another locker room payday.

The series finished as it had started, with little competition and victories against teams from St. John's and the Newfoundland All-stars. The game against St. John's had a final score of 10-8, with one local paper describing Faulkner's team as "noticeably holding back." At the end of the second period, the St. John's lads were actually leading by one goal. St. John's players Charlie Walsh, "Blondie" Bartlett and "Fa" Murphy had two goals each, with Cy Hoskins and veteran Jackie Withers getting the others.

The game against the so-called Newfoundland All-stars, with players representing their teams from all areas of the island, did not materialize as expected. Many players originally chosen could not make it into St. John's for the game, and substitutes from the local league had to fill in. The top line was from the central area: Alex Faulkner, Hugh Wadden and Bucky Hannaford. "Sham" McInnis made it in from Grand Falls to play goal and had an outstanding night against the pros. The final score showed another easy win for the visitors, however: 14-6.

The local press had kept a close eye on George throughout, and were certainly impressed by what they saw. In Grand Falls, one reporter wrote that he saw a 50 percent improvement in his skating – a much faster skater had emerged from the pro ranks than anyone had expected. Sports writers and players alike were overwhelmed with the Quebecers' passing skills, their puck control in offensive play, and the ease with which they patterned their puck-clearing moves in their own zone. But it was the speed they showed each time that got the most notice – and generated the most intimidation for the competition. As for our own players at the time, the Quebecers always spoke of their great spirit and desire to win. What they lacked in speed and hockey skills, they made up for in pure grit.

The end result of the hockey experience gained, coming from all quarters of that tour, was clearly the need for more professional coaching, such as Grand Falls, Buchans and, more recently, Bell Island had acquired with the signing of Joe Byrne, George Faulkner's coach and mentor from his first years in Quebec.

The Quebec All-stars returned home immediately after the tour ended. George flew on to New York to join Midge for a few days before the couple returned to Shawinigan to put domestic matters in order for the summer. As in other years, the question of where the future might take them was once again up in the air – another waiting period until the end of the summer to see if anything had changed, and whether there would be another invitation to play hockey in Quebec. He was now 24 years old and reaching his peak as a hockey player. Beyond the mid-20s everyone knew the call to play in the NHL grew more unlikely. One by one, longtime teammates began to move away. Eddie Kachur had moved on to play in Chicago, and his closest friend, 25-year-old Connie Broden, was already considering retirement. More important things in his world had to be considered that spring as well: Midge was now pregnant with their first child, due that summer, adding a completely different focus on their plans for the future.

Shortly after the tour began, George did an interview with the St. John's daily *The Evening Telegram*, in which he revealed what appeared to be some definite plans for the future. He told the reporter quite openly that he looked forward to his coming back home after the next year in Quebec, if the right opportunity came along – a playing-coach proposition, for example. Going further in that interview, he expressed the view for the first time that his chances of making it to the NHL were getting fewer and fewer. He would soon be starting his fourth year as a professional hockey player tied to an organization that was getting stronger and stronger; in fact, dominating the entire league which it could continue to do for the next while. He had been overlooked several times in the last few years and began to see little chance of that situation ever changing, at least with Montreal. Realistically, it was indeed time to look elsewhere.

No doubt, hockey moguls in the Newfoundland set-up that spring knew from that interview what was coming, and the prospect of capturing a professional "son" no less would be the golden egg for any community. By the end of the 1957-58 season, that golden egg would appear in the already brimming hockey basket of the Moores family and its new arena in Conception Bay.

11

THE FINAL YEAR

ON ONE OF THOSE HOT SUMMER AFTERNOONS IN AUGUST 1957, along the highway leading into the small but busy seaport of Botwood, George Faulkner and a few friends were busy pouring a concrete basement for a member of the family– a full day's work, which they'd started early that morning. Around six o'clock that afternoon, his father, Lester, pulled up in his pickup, walked over and told him, "You've got a hockey player down in the hospital in Botwood." Lester stood there beaming but said nothing more.

The call had come around lunch hour that Midge was ready, and Lester and company, not wanting to bother George with his work that day, simply took her aboard the truck and headed directly to see Dr. Hugh Thomey at the cottage hospital in Botwood. Shortly thereafter, Robert John Faulkner looked out at his new world, a dark-haired little fellow with long black sideburns. There was not the slightest sign of the blond, curly locks of the Faulkner's Swedish side. "I didn't grasp it at first. He was so dark. Then I realized how he was dark like his mother. In the confusion of the moment, I looked at my father standing next to me, and I remember saying, 'Boy, he's some hard-looking.'" Lester just looked at him.

George doesn't remember if he finished pouring concrete that day or not, but it was after supper before he got to see the little guy, and long after that before he told Midge of his first reaction.

Training camp was barely a month away. It was shortly after Robert's birth that he received word from Montreal to report for another year in Shawinigan. The camp was held once again at the Montreal Forum. The routine, and the salary, were much the same: no increase again this year, and playoff money, if they were lucky enough to make it that far, the same as well. It was still a handsome and livable wage for the time, but with the arrival of their first child, a little addition to the pot would have helped.

There was the familiar separate dressing and training facilities for the Canadiens and the Cataracts, the same inter-squad competitions, and, most of all, those continuing opportunities to be juggled about on various lines with the veteran Canadiens stars. George soon recognized considerable changes in the 1957-58 Shawinigan lineup. Connie Broden thought seriously of retiring from the sport altogether that year, but when offered the chance to play for Canada with the Whitby Dunlops in the World Hockey Tournament, he reconsidered and jumped at the chance to play at the international level.

Along with Broden and Kachur, and two of last year's goalies – Bob Perreault and Charlie Hodge – at least a dozen players were missing from the team that had ignominiously finished in last place the year before. The new faces would include linemates Al Johnson and Ron Attwell, goalie Eddie Johnston* and 31-year-old playing-coach Fred Shero. Shero had spent three years with the New York Rangers as a player, but had logged most of his career in the minor systems. The 1957-58 season would be his last in that capacity. Under Shero's unique and sometimes philosophical coaching style, the Cataracts would bounce back to become contenders once again in the QHL.

George liked Shero from the very beginning. "He was pretty good at matching players on a line – getting the most out of the right combinations. He was a good coach, played in the NHL, a mild, mild man. He didn't have very much to say. Some coaches would bawl you out, shame you in a lot of ways, or sometimes call you into their office, but he never ever did that with us." Certainly Fred Shero had his ways. But it would take almost a lifetime of minor league coaching before his strange yet highly successful coaching system and game tactics would show themselves at the NHL level. Working with the Shawinigan Cataracts this year was just one more learning experience along the way, but for George Faulkner, it was to be a memorable one.

---

* Eddie Johnston would spend 16 seasons as an NHL goalie – 11 with Boston and 5 with the St. Louis Blues. He played back-up goalie to Ken Dryden during the famous Summit Series against Russia in 1972, but was not used in any of the eight games.

Many hockey experts from those years, and perhaps just as many today, often talk about the 1958 Montreal Canadiens as probably the best team ever assembled, despite the number of injuries and player losses that came their way that year: "Boom Boom" Geoffrion, Dickie Moore, Henri Richard, Jacques Plante, Jean-Guy Talbot, Bert Olmstead, Donnie Marshall, Floyd Curry, Dollard St. Laurent and, most seriously of all, "Rocket" Richard, who missed three full months of play. Call-ups from the various minor league teams, and several in particular from Shawinigan, came on a regular basis. At one point, with the two Richard brothers out, there was talk around the Montreal hockey world that a third brother, Claude,* might finally break into the Canadiens' lineup. Claude played for the Ottawa-Hull Junior Canadiens at the time and had several tryouts with the team during his young career. He was 16 years younger than Maurice and one behind Henri, and was in many ways a skillful and dynamic player in his own right. Despite his consistently strong playing effort and notable scoring statistics each year, he was not destined to join his more famous brothers at the NHL level, even during the club's most trying, injury-riddled season. Had he made it to Montreal, no one knows what lucrative paydays and exciting games the masterful Richard trio would have brought to the organization and to the league itself. Instead, the Canadiens' call-ups went to more skilled players like Billy Hicke, Ralph Backstrom, Murray Balfour,** Charlie Hodge and Ab McDonald, all of whom would enjoy lengthy careers in the top professional ranks.

Whatever coaching magic Fred Shero brought to the Shawinigan dressing room that year took hold right from the start: five consecutive wins, including goalie Eddie Johnston's first shutout in this new league. By month's end the team was

---

* Fans already had Maurice "the Rocket," and Henri "the Pocket Rocket," so the name many chose for young Claude Richard was "the Socket Pocket Rocket" – which didn't really make much sense, except for the rhyme. The wiser and more imaginative people in the Montreal press preferred the epithet: "the Vest Pocket Rocket," which perhaps had a little more zip to it.

** Murray Balfour spent six years in the NHL, five of them with the Chicago Blackhawks. Best known as a member of Chicago's "Million Dollar Line," with Bobby Hull and Billy "Red" Hay, Balfour's career was cut short because of lung problems. He died in Regina on May 30, 1965. He was 28 years old.

holding first place with a 5-2-1 record for 11 points. George began the season almost as successfully, with a two-goal performance in the first game and seven points on the month's score sheet. The rejuvenated Shawinigan hockey world was already "turning as it should."

The month of November proved a more difficult one for the club. Their record fell below the .500 level in won-lost games. It seemed the only team they could beat with any consistency was the Montreal Royals, but even the Royals took a piece out of them late in the month, with a 4-0 shellacking.

Eddie Johnston replaced Claude Pronovost in December, and there were high hopes for his goaltending gymnastics to carry them near the top for the rest of the season. It seemed the pundits were right, at least for a while. Johnston led the team to six straight unbeaten games, including two shutouts. It was not until December 22 that their unbeaten string came to an end. At the end of December, they were still in second place in the standings and were the highest-scoring team in the league, with 107 goals.

Very little changed for the rest of the season. Eddie Johnston's sparkling start to the year soon faded, with inconsistent performances. According to press reports, Eddie could never be relied on to perform the same way game after game. At times, he could be spectacular; at other times, anything but. The evidence of the team's record through January and February tells the same story: the team would lose four straight, then win six in a row, or combine an exciting run of three wins followed by four straight losses. Nevertheless, at the end of February they held second place, with a 28-23-4 record and 62 points, and seemed destined for another shot at the playoffs, their third in four years.

Meanwhile, George moved along at his usual steady pace, garnering mostly assists but putting together several two-goal games, and one exciting game-tying goal with three seconds left in the game against the Trois Rivières Lions on February 17. The knee problems he seemed to encounter each year came back in early January, but they were not serious enough to keep him out for any length of time. Shawinigan's new line of Johnson-Faulkner-Attwell was making its presence known throughout the league and getting its share of attention in the press. George continued to be the leading goal-scorer of the three, a point that would carry over into the playoffs, when their line was highlighted game after game as leaders on the team. It seemed fitting that in his final professional year, George Faulkner was proving once again that he was among the best in the QHL. The last month of the season had its moments. The Cataracts continued their hot-and-cold pattern, but this time without a winning flourish to carry them. Luckily, the same could be said of the Montreal Royals and Quebec Aces, unable to make up any ground that month and destined to finish third and fourth respectively, behind Chicoutimi and Shawinigan.

On March 4, as the Cataracts were beating the Quebec Aces, 4-3, the country turned its attention almost fully to the World Ice Hockey Tournament starting that day in Oslo, Norway. The Whitby Dunlops, with Connie Broden and company, had literally demolished the competition in exhibition play before the tournament began. Along with retired Toronto Maple Leaf star Sid Smith, the team captain that year, Broden would go on to lead the tournament in scoring and to the World Hockey Championship. Broden's play in that tournament would win him his second invitation to play with the Montreal Canadiens in the playoffs for the Stanley Cup.

As dismal and unexciting as was the Cataracts' play during that final month, it would get even worse. On March 16, the nomads of Quebec hockey, the "Baby Habs," were in town for an exhibition game. The surprising outcome was a humiliating 5-2 loss for the Cataracts, while Claude Richard, the star-crossed "Vest Pocket Rocket," would add to the insult with a nicely timed hat trick. As if that wasn't enough of a lesson, their final game of the season, on March 23, saw them lose to the arch-rival Montreal Royals, the team they had beaten all year, and the one they were about to face in the first game of the playoffs in three days' time. As expected, the semi-final series would produce the most exciting hockey either team had played all year.

Just as it does today, making it to the payoffs – the so-called "second season" – meant extra paydays and bigger purses and the kind of instant recognition you couldn't get in the regular season: a chance to become more famous than you already were. You only have to think back to some very big playoff moments in sport and the names that made them famous: hockey's Bill Barilko, baseballer's Don Larsen and Bill Mazeroski, to name a few from that era. In the spring of 1958, realizing that it might well be his last year in the professional ranks, George Faulkner was already playing his best hockey and thinking ahead – like everyone else. This might possibly be his last playoffs as a professional. If nothing else, at least there was the additional money to be had. In the case of coach Fred Shero, it was the same, except the payout for him – what he thought was a well-kept secret all season long – was known from the outset and was about to be celebrated.

George remembered how members of the team had learned of Shero's salary arrangement around the time the season began, even though it was never made public. "We knew about the set-up all season long but never said anything about the chance he was taking with us that last year. As playing coach, he agreed to a salary of $100 a week, less than even we were making at the time. He probably could have been making $250 a week but he opted for an arrangement that showed not only his belief in himself, but in us as well: he'd work for only $100 a week, but if we made the playoffs he'd get a bonus of $6,000! We made the playoffs, and he got his $6,000, plus an extra $100 a week during the playoffs. The average NHL salary for first-year players that year was $7,500. Most might have made $8,000, unless you were a Jean Beliveau ..."

Maybe Shero's thinking was simply this: what were the chances of being among the top four teams at playoff time in a five-team league? It was still a gamble, but the odds were certainly in his favour. Perhaps the gamble was really more about stature and prestige than simply financial gain. Whatever the real reason for the move, it certainly gave the 1958 Shawinigan Cataracts all the more reason to want to win this time round.

There would be no one-sided betting either way on the outcome of the 1958 QHL playoffs. The four teams – Chicoutimi, Shawinigan, Montreal and Quebec – were balanced equally in every respect. In the league's 68-game schedule, a mere six-point game differential was all that separated top from bottom. Both semi-final and finals would be best of seven.

Surprisingly, first-place Chicoutimi would be first to bow out, losing four games to none to the Quebec Aces. The Royals-Cataracts encounter would go the limit. Shawinigan eased through the first two games at home. In game three, the Cataracts led 6-2 at one point, only to lose 8-7 in overtime. The Royals came back to win by a single goal in game four as well: 4-3. Both were home games for the Royals.

While Shawinigan continued to win by one goal (they took game five by a 3-2 score), the Royals would come back once again in game six with a humiliating 5-0 rout. Game seven was set for Shawinigan on Sunday afternoon, April 13, and, almost as if it had been scripted, it would be Shawinigan once again by one goal. This time, however, the pattern of the game was entirely different. The Cataracts struck with two goals in the first two minutes, out-shooting the Royals overall, but saved in the third period by the unpredictable Eddie Johnston, this time rising to the occasion and moving the team on to the QHL finals. The *Montreal Gazette* described Shawinigan's first goal:

> The line of Ron Attwell, Allan Johnson and George Faulkner stormed to the attack from the opening faceoff and came up with a goal in 54 seconds of play. Attwell blazed down left wing, took a pass from Faulkner at the blueline and cut into the defence before letting go with a successful 25-foot drive.

Faulkner's line had led the way in this round of the playoffs, gathering a total of 18 points in all, and there was more to come.

The QHL finals would be almost a repeat of what had just happened in the semi-finals. Shawinigan would open at home with a win – a goal at 10:18 of the first overtime by George Faulkner, assisted by Ron Attwell. It seems the loss was more than a shock to fans of the Aces. The *Quebec Chronicle-Telegraph* of April 16 reacted this way: "... the Cats are a group of skating fools."

It would be the start of another home-and-home winning affair: the Cataracts winning by one goal each time (three in overtime) at home, and Quebec winning by a three-goal margin in each of its games at the Quebec Colisée. In game seven, in Shawinigan, the pattern would be the same: the Cataracts winning 6-5 in overtime, coming back from a two-goal deficit at the end of the second period, and led once again by Attwell, Johnson and Faulkner, with four of the team's points that day.

Fittingly, it would be George's last championship as a pro, and his sixth in six professional years, including the double victories in 1954-55: the QHL and Canadian Championship (Edinburgh Trophy).

The 1957-58 season would be the last for the Shawinigan Cataracts as well. The team was disbanded at the end of that year by its owners, the Montreal Canadiens' organization. In fact, the Quebec Hockey League itself would survive only one more year, the 1958-59 season. It had been reduced to a four-team league after the loss of the Cataracts, and at the end of 1959 the entire league shut down in favour of a new entity, the Eastern Professional Hockey League, which operated until 1963.

George knew nothing of the plan to drop the Cataracts when he left for home at the end of the season. The news came during the summer that the Montreal organization, which owned the entire league, had been planning the move for awhile and would stay with the QHL set-up for just one more year.

He knew by now that he would never make the Montreal Canadiens, but that his future in hockey was still in their hands. Who knows, he was thinking, what might develop over the summer? Would they finally release him if a call came from another NHL team? Would he be invited to play with one of the four remaining semi-pro Quebec teams? For now, another season had passed and it was time again, along with Midge and young Robert, to get back home.

1958-66

PART THREE

THE NEWFOUNDLAND GAME

1958-1966

12

A HOME IN HARBOUR GRACE

By the time Freddie Shero's letter arrived later that summer with an offer
to play in Sault Ste. Marie, I'd already pretty well closed the deal with the Moores
family in Harbour Grace. No one could match their offer, financially or otherwise.
I would be making NHL money back home in a job made to order for me and
my family. I knew I was home for good.*

FAR FROM THE CLUTTER OF HOCKEY DRESSING ROOMS
and the cold arenas of Quebec, the summer of 1958 would be work-free for the
Faulkner family, and for the first time would allow frequent travel by means of a
family car: a 1953 maroon Mercury, newly acquired from a friend of Lester
Faulkner for $1,100. The visits to the community of Howley, Midge's home,
could now be taken along the dirt roads of Newfoundland's interior as far as
Deer Lake. They'd park the car in Deer Lake, then have to backtrack a few miles
by train into the small lumber town. "The Mercury gave a good, smooth ride on
the dirt roads. She was heavy enough so's you could sail along comfortably on
those long trips."

Howley was a twenty-minute run by train east of Deer Lake, and the ride
always added a bit more of an adventure to their trip, as if the dust and potholes
of the province's roads weren't enough. The time spent in Howley was pure

---

* Shero wrote George in late summer with an offer to play in a semi-professional league that year
in northern Ontario. The offer was at the same pay as he'd received the year before in the QHL.

leisure time – trouting in the rich surrounding waters and berrypicking along the shores of Sandy Lake and Grand Lake. "We'd stay in Howley as long as we wanted. We had no schedules to live by, nothing to interrupt our stay. In late summer, when the trouting season was winding down, and the blueberries were beginning to ripen, we'd cross the trussel that spanned the narrows from Grand Lake into Sandy Lake and hike further inland. Up there we'd go off the track a ways, and find blueberries as big as grapes."

Life on the return to Bishop's Falls was taken up by endless soccer activities in the local leagues – a tougher exercise regimen than even hockey.

Sometime in late July, with hockey still furthest from his mind, George happened to meet Joe Byrne, his old coach and friend from earlier days in Grand Falls. Byrne had since taken over hockey activities on Bell Island, managing the town's busy arena but always keeping in touch with old friends in Bishop's Falls and Grand Falls. The conversation was hardly underway when the topic turned to what the next step in George's future might be. Byrne knew – from what he'd read the previous year in the *Evening Telegram* article – that George might be interested in a hockey future here at home.

"There's a new stadium just opened in Harbour Grace, owned by the Moores family over there," Joe explained. "They already have a guy hired to manage the place but they'd certainly be looking for someone to run the hockey program. They'd probably jump at the chance to get someone with your background. You should look into it right away."

Midge seemed enthusiastic about the idea and remembered a student-nursing friend who lived in nearby Brigus. Gladys Yeats, now married to a school teacher from the area, John Leaman, was contacted, told of their Harbour Grace plans, and the trip to Conception Bay and the East Coast was underway. George remembers thinking at the time: "I didn't even know where Brigus was."

Leaman was teaching music in the neighbouring town of Carbonear, and knowing the value to any town's hockey program that someone like Faulkner could bring, he decided he'd introduce George to his own people first. Carbonear did not have its own stadium back then, so there was not much enthusiasm for getting a full-time person just for hockey. Harbour Grace, it turned out, was still the best bet.

Lloyd Archibald of Archibald Farms arranged the first meeting with the manager of the Harbour Grace Stadium, Lorne Wakelin, a former manager of the Memorial Stadium in St. John's. Wakelin knew enough about hockey and the name "George Faulkner" to want to explore the prospects without delay, and he set up a meeting with a member of the stadium's board of directors that same day. He knew firsthand what an NAHA franchise could do for the town and the whole Conception Bay area. They would have the best of both worlds: a 24-year-old playing-coach and former professional hockey player for the town's hockey setup and, given a year-round position, someone quite capable of organizing the town's recreation program. The meeting had hardly begun when, as George recalled, "Lorne got up from the desk and suggested we go down to the Moores' premises and meet the boss of the plant and the new stadium. Things were happening that fast. I'll never forget it. This young guy comes out of a little office attached to the fish plant, wearing wet knee rubbers and an old jacket and is bawling orders at everybody and everything around him: fishermen unloading catches onto the wharf, boats and crews coming and going, wheelbarrows of fish rolling by, with fish trailings falling all over the place. Meantime, he's got this big smile going all the time. He looked just like one of the guys."

Frank Moores* hardly stopped long enough to know they were there. After a quick handshake to both visitors, he beckons and says, "Come on up to the office."

No more to it than that.

The brief meeting that followed with Moores was as casual and friendly as had been the introductions a few minutes before. "Frank Moores was an incredibly likeable man. No artificial mannerisms of any kind. As outgoing and down-to-earth then as he was years later when he became premier of the province." George remembers thinking how easy it would be to work for a man like this. It seems the feelings between the two were mutual. Moores called for a board of directors' session that night and invited George along as well. "I didn't sit in on the meeting, but they had me wait around outside. It felt like the position might be mine."

---

* Frank Moores (1933-2005) served as Premier of Newfoundland from 1972-1979.

Led by Moores, the board of directors – Lo Pike, Lloyd Archibald, Ned Oake, Dr. Roy Goodwin and M.P. Stapleton – discussed the possibilities of Faulkner's employment as a kind of recreation director and how the position might work hand-in-hand with that of Stadium Manager Lorne Wakelin. The two men could work side-by-side in handling the community's recreational and business affairs in that area. Wakelin's was a full-time position at the stadium, and the committee saw Faulkner's in the same way. It would mean a year-round involvement in recreational matters: hockey at all levels during the winter – including playing-coach for their NAHA entry – and organizing and overseeing summer sports, such as soccer and softball. The salary proposed was $6,500, a considerable jump for George from the previous year and one close to what he might have made in NHL terms. A bonus was laid out as well: if he was interested in handling an annual crafts fair at the stadium – The Trinity-Conception Home Crafts Exhibition – the committee would add an extra $1,500 to his income.

Everything seemed to be happening so fast, all in this one meeting, but he knew immediately the workload ahead was as much as any one individual could handle. It was, too, a world largely different from anything he was used to. On the return trip home he kept thinking and talking of what it all meant – the leadership required, the organizing abilities needed, the hard work to come and the new lifestyle that would soon come his way. Midge quickly put it all back in perspective for him: "At least you'll still be playing hockey."

The move to Harbour Grace came about during the first week in September. The big '53 Mercury once again rolled off Joey Hampton's "scow" on the Exploits River, and the Faulkners were on their way. They had the good fortune to find a small three-bedroom bungalow on Cathedral Street for the grand sum of forty dollars a month, compliments once again of his new employers. Midge seemed delighted with her new surroundings and the chance to live in one place for a change and to have George off the road for the first time. The house seemed made to order. A healthy young Robert was moving into his second year, and she would soon learn how wonderful and welcoming the people of Harbour Grace and area could be. George, on the other hand, was wondering, "Where do I start?"

13

THE FIRST GAME

HIS FIRST ROLE WAS TO ORGANIZE SENIOR HOCKEY.
Next, to round up a team to represent the area in NAHA competition –
possibly have them ready in a year, or maybe two years' time. It was Frank
Moores' idea to bring in Newfoundlanders from outside who didn't have a job
but wanted a job. "Outsiders" dominated NAHA play in those years, mostly
coming from the Maritimes, with a few from Quebec – journeymen hockey
players paid to bolster local teams and bring home the Herder Memorial
Trophy to their community.

NAHA league competition began in late October, giving George some
time to have a first look at what talent was available locally, but not thinking
he'd have a team, or anything close to a team, to compete in the 1958 season. "I
called an open practice, and I called Bob Cole at VOCM in St. John's to put it
on their sportscast. I was looking forward to it because the area had had its own
senior league operating for some years – teams from Carbonear, Upper Island
Cove, Bay Roberts, Shearstown, Brigus and Harbour Grace."

About 50 or 60 guys showed up for that first practice; only a few of them
had any "proper" hockey equipment, the ones who knew enough about the game
to come prepared for the tryout. "The rest just had their skates and a hockey
stick. They were up in the bleachers putting on their skates – instead of in
the dressing room. All they had were those wool socks with the red tops –
something like the fishermen used to wear, I suppose – knee-high wool socks,
home-spun, hauled up over their pants, up to their knees, with the red tops
showing. And worsted mitts for hockey gloves. I wish I'd had a camera at the

time. Can you imagine twenty players coming on the ice, all at the same time, dressed like that? It was a sight to behold, but, thinking back to it now, a nice part of the history of the time and the game."

The better and more seasoned players came fully equipped and looked pretty good when they got on the ice: the Penneys from Carbonear; Neville Pike, John Thomey and Frank Fleming from Harbour Grace; Wes Gosse from Spaniard's Bay; Allan Dawe from Coley's Point; Tom and Graham Sparkes from Shearstown; Dave and George Jerrett and "Rocket" Ed Hayes from Brigus.

When it seemed to George that he had enough players for the makings of a team, including brother Alex and Jimmy Kennedy from Bishop's Falls who both had signed on at the plant around the same time, he set up routine practice times: 6:30 p.m. to 8:00 p.m., Monday to Friday, and an additional hour for those who could make it at 11:00 a.m. each morning: an ample amount of practice time to get a team in shape, and just maybe, ready for competition of some kind.

It wasn't long before word got around that George Faulkner had settled in Harbour Grace and was building a team for NAHA competition. The first interesting call came from his old alma mater in Grand Falls. Jimmy Pond, manager of the Grand Falls Stadium, called with an invitation for an exhibition game to be played in Grand Falls around the end of November. George remembers his reaction to the invite: "I knew myself and Alex and Jimmy Kennedy would welcome it because we'd get a chance to look at the Grand Falls team, but I didn't say anything to the team just yet – didn't want to scare them to death in the first weeks or so. It was still in the back of my mind that we might have a team ready for competition this year." He recalled a conversation with Frank Moores earlier in which Moores had made it clear that NAHA competition was certainly one year away, maybe two. George said nothing either way.

He held off on telling the team until after the next practice, when they had all gathered in the team dressing room: "I had a phone call before practice tonight. Jimmy Pond wants us to go into Grand Falls to play the first game of the season, an exhibition game. Before you say anything, he also wants to play the game this Saturday – a few days from now. What do you think?"

Nobody said a word. There was a long silence.

Finally, someone said, "What do you think? If you think we're okay to go in, we'll do it."

The Grand Falls Andcos* was the dominant NAHA team at the time, winning four straight Herder championships, 1955-58, and had their share of mainland players in the lineup. It seemed a lot to ask of any team to want to take them on in their home rink in the first game of the season. The one thing George knew his squad would have going for them was conditioning. After more than two full weeks of tight, exhausting skating drills – hopping the circles, forwards and backwards sessions, figure eights, stops and starts, dropping to their knees and up and going again – the team finally began to show signs of shaping up. "That's the main reason we took them on," George explained. "We were in shape, and we knew the longer the game went on, the better chances we had." The only thing left was the financial arrangements and even here, the Harbour Grace lads came out okay: a 60-40 arrangement on the gate (the higher portion going to Harbour Grace), a gate that would reflect a full house that night. The game was scheduled for Saturday, November 25, at 8:30 p.m.

Faulkner's team arrived just before game time to find a huge crowd lined up outside the stadium. They muscled their way through the crowd to get to their dressing room, hardly believing the size of the turnout. A crowd of 2,400 was tallied that night, second only to the 2,600 who had come out to see a New York Rangers exhibition game earlier that year. Lloyd Andrews, the Harbour Grace team manager, was appointed ticket scrutineer that night, with the task of running back and forth from the dressing room to the turnstiles every few minutes, keeping tabs as best he could on the night's ticket sales. The 60-percent promised gate was his responsibility, a way of ensuring they had covered all game possibilities, apart from the outcome itself. In real life, Lloyd was the keen-eyed – some would say "hawk-eyed" – observer at the fish plant's weigh scales, responsible for every pound that came and went through the yard. Counting ticket-holders, he said, was a bit more difficult. Finally, when things were ready to go, he came into the dressing room for the final time and announced: "Boys, there's a fine crowd out there. We're blocking 'em in. We'll have a nice bit of money when we get back home to start off the season with, and maybe enough for a free one on the way."

---

* The team was named after its sponsor, the Anglo-Newfoundland Development Company, which owned and operated the Grand Falls paper mill.

Back then, the local arenas had no sound system to indicate game time. Instead, there was that shrill sound of the referee's whistle outside the dressing room door. A startling moment for any team, but especially for the young crew from Conception Bay on that evening. During the pre-game skate, one of his players, Jimmy Penney, a bit of a character with a dry sense of humour, skated up to George, pointed to an oversized giant on the Grand Falls squad dancing around the net, and asked: "Who's that big fellow over there? Am I supposed to guard him?" The "big fellow" was Terry Jesseau, at right defence, who would play opposite the left-shooting Penney on each shift. "Do you mean to tell me I've got to go into the corner with him?" Penney continued, still in awe of big Jesseau. "You won't have to go in the corner with him too many times," George told him. "He might be a bit frisky the first shift or so, but he won't be that way for long, because I'm going to take care of him." George obviously had seen plenty of "big fellows" in his time and knew the routine.

Grand Falls sports columnist Roger Howse, a noted sportsman and sports analyst, predicted the Andcos would win by five goals. He acknowledged the powerful Faulkners as probably being a force throughout the game, but felt the Andcos, in balance and experience, would overcome the team from Conception Bay. The game was barely minutes old when Alex Faulkner broke in, had his shot blocked by goalie Mun Pond, only to have brother Lindy swoop in on the rebound for the goal. Lindy, it seems, still working and living at home in Bishop's Falls, had decided to play with the family. It was, after all, just an exhibition game, and most likely the fans would love to see the Faulkners together again. Young Brian Wakelin, barely out of the minor hockey system and playing on a line with Alex and Lindy, scored their second goal.

The score was tied 2-2 at the end of the second period, and the final score had Conception Bay over the Andcos by 7-4. "The Cinderella squad"* had done the impossible, and the Faulkners even more so. They were in on all seven goals, gathering 14 points: Alex with three goals and three assists, Lindy was one and five, and George, now playing defence full time, had two.

---

* The roster of that first Conception Bay All-star team: George Faulkner, Murray Matheson, Alex Faulkner, Lindy Faulkner, Brian Wakelin, Len Williams, Jim Coady, Fred Williams, Neville Pike, Carl Penney, Fred Rossiter, Jim Penney, Reg Parsons and John Thomey.

A standout among the crowd that night was team owner Frank Moores, but on this occasion looking more like its mascot, making his rounds of the stadium in a light-colored topcoat festooned on the back with flags and buttons of all makes and sizes; in fact, covering the entire back surface. He made a visit to the team dressing room before the game to show off the coat, and, after the game was over, jumped on the ice to congratulate them, topcoat flying as he slipped his way from player to player in a wild victory celebration. Everyone was thinking the same thing: the trip back home would be one to remember.

As they left the ice, with Frank Moores in tow, the team received a standing ovation. In the media next day, they were being described as the "powerful Harbour Grace team." It seemed George might be right: maybe they could ice a team for this year's NAHA competition after all.

The people of Conception Bay, especially those living in the team's hometown of Harbour Grace, took to the Ceebees from the moment of the first faceoff.

No one remotely thought a team could be brought together so quickly, and certainly not one so competitive as to take on the mighty Grand Falls Andcos of 1958.

Neighbouring towns, long established with their own league, playing year after year on outdoor rinks, flocked to the new stadium for every game.

Hockey fans from Coley's Point, Shearstown, Spaniard's Bay, and Carbonear showed up in the hundreds, just to watch their team practice.

The game brought new life to the Bay, its people suddenly part of the mosaic of Canadian hockey. For the next decade, their Ceebees would always be on the threshold of victory, no matter what the opposition.

The excitement of finally watching hometown hockey was matched only by the excitement of seeing the Faulkners play: skating, checking, precision passing, stickhandling, shooting. Amazing displays at every game.

The next day you could maybe drop by the local fish plant, chat with Frank Moores about last night's game, or maybe stroll by George's place, and ask: "Whadd'ya think of the game last night?"

There was always somebody around willing to talk hockey.

1954 QUEBEC CITADELLES. (Junior "A" Champions) Coach Phil ("Fiery Phil") Watson congratulates team members after a victory over a team from Cap-de-la-Madeleine. Leo Amadio stands behind Watson. George is partially hidden behind Ray Cyr, wearing "A."

THE THREE MUSKETEERS would spend three full years together in Shawinigan-Falls as teammates and roommates. Broden and Kachur had short shifts in the NHL, but, like George, would spend most of their careers in the minor professional system.

THE FIRST TRAINING CAMP WITH VETERAN KENNY MOSDELL AND COACH DICK IRVIN. Irvin lost out on a bid to sign George to an NHL contract (along with Connie Broden and Claude Provost) when he left the Canadiens in 1955 to take over coaching duties with the lowly Chicago Blackhawks.

"THE ROCKET WAS SO FAMOUS IN THOSE YEARS … there was really no one like him. Everyone in camp knew he was a quiet, unassuming person, and didn't care much for all the attention. The morning this picture was taken, there was a break in the practice routine, and I simply skated over and asked him if we could get together at the boards for a quick shot for the folks back home. He almost smiled."

THE FIRST YEAR. Playing coach Roger Leger is shown holding the Edinburgh Trophy, (Canadian Professional Championship) after his Shawinigan-Falls Cataracts defeated the Edmonton Flyers. Some prominent faces: (back row: Left to right - Eddie Kachur, Connie Broden, George; second row: Claude Provost (2nd left); Bob Turner and Jean-Guy Talbot (6th and 7th from left); goalie Bob Perreault, seated far right.

14

THE CONCEPTION BAY ALL-STARS

AT ITS INCEPTION, THE NAHA "RESIDENT RULE" WAS A simple one: residency was required as of November 1 each year. It didn't matter where you lived on November 2, you were still eligible to play for the community in which you were housed on that first day of the month. After the All-stars' impressive win against Grand Falls in that famous November 1958 exhibition game, the league had enough sense to see the damaging possibilities in the player residency requirement – a clear overloading of talent in any one community, while its players lived elsewhere.

In the case of George Faulkner's All-stars, the old rule would have allowed brother Lindy to play with Conception Bay during the 1958-59 season, while still living and working as a family man in his hometown of Bishop's Falls – a neat weekend arrangement for himself and the team. "We needed Lindy to play with us. He'd played with Grand Falls teams for years, and we thought at the beginning of the year that he would be playing with us, because Lindy was in Harbour Grace on November 1, which satisfied the residency rule as it stood at the time."

Lindy continued to play with the All-stars until around December 14, when the semi-annual meeting of the NAHA Executive changed the rule. The executive confronted the obvious and changed the residency requirement immediately, affecting the status of several players in 1958, who now had to live and find work, i.e., "had to remain" in the community they played for. The rule went into effect immediately and Lindy Faulkner, only 28, was gone from the All-stars' roster. Neither does his name appear on the Grand Falls roster that year, nor for many years thereafter.

As expected, Faulkner's All-stars and the Grand Falls Andcos dominated the 1958-59 Herder Cup schedule and wound up as contenders for the cup in April that season.

Before that would happen, a wild encounter during a game in Grand Falls in February would see the All-stars players leave the ice mid-way through the third period over a disputed call against Alex Faulkner – a series of penalties coming together against the star player at a crucial point in the game. With the score tied at 5-5, George called his team to the box to get their reaction, and promptly left for the dressing room. After a series of attempts by the referee to get them to continue, with no result, he called a penalty shot into an empty net against them. The Andcos were given the win by a 6-5 score, one of the first losses for that year.

Another loss occurred in one of their many exhibition games, in a contest against the visiting Ottawa-Hull Junior Canadiens, an old adversary of George's from the previous year as a Quebec professional. The Junior Canadiens were on a short tour of the province in November 1958, with games in Corner Brook, Grand Falls and Gander. The young Quebec professionals demolished the competition in these first games but were to receive quite a surprise in the game against the Conception Bay All-stars. Here the French squad would find themselves in a familiar setting – a tough, competitive hockey game. The All-stars – the new upstarts in Newfoundland hockey – fought the Canadiens for three exciting periods, finally losing 10-6. Alex Faulkner scored all six goals for Conception Bay, while George played all sixty minutes of the game. A reporter commented next day that "when George Faulkner came off the ice after playing all sixty minutes, he looked like he could still play another sixty!"

Among the Junior Canadiens lineup that day were future NHLers Jacques Laperrière and Keith McCreary. There's an interesting footnote to hockey history in the NHL connected to the name McCreary, more mythical than factual, but one that did the rounds in its day and still leaves a touch of intrigue in the minds of many as to what actually transpired.

Keith McCreary's nephew, Bill McCreary Jr., followed in the McCreary family footsteps* and made it to the NHL in 1980-81 as a member of the

---

* Bill McCreary Sr., older brother of Keith McCreary, played for four NHL teams and went on later to coach the NHL's Vancouver Canucks.

Toronto Maple Leafs. He played a total of 12 games in the NHL, and is most remembered for what he did in of his brief career, a game the Leafs lost to Edmonton, 4-1. McCreary flattened Wayne Gretzky in a clean "open ice hit." The video of the incident shows Gretzky about to cross the Leafs' blueline, head down, when McCreary makes the hit, as frightening a moment as you'd ever see in hockey. It then shows Gretzky slowly collapsing to the ice, lying flat on his back, in what clearly appears to be a critical moment for the young Edmonton superstar.*

Naturally, the incident caused quite a stir next day in many of Canada's newspapers, making McCreary's name instantly recognizable: he was the guy who'd almost put an end to the career of "The Great One." Instead, it was McCreary himself who would disappear from hockey history – almost overnight. Bill McCreary went on to play only ten more games in the NHL. While the myth that had him never playing another game in the NHL is clearly wrong, it's safe to say he never played another one against Gretzky.

To some, Bill McCreary's NHL playing record might look like something you'd see on a headstone – graphic and complete:

First Game – December 30, 1980.
Last Game – January 30, 1981.

No one has ever offered an explanation as to why the 20-year-old would never again play in the NHL. We can only guess.

George takes great pride in the kind of discipline he imposed on his players throughout his coaching years. He made the rules clear with every team, and was seldom placed in a position to have to take action. One such incident happened during an overnight train trip to Corner Brook. The offence, by today's standards, seems laughable; but it shows how seriously he wanted to be ready for every game.

Shortly after the team headed for their sleeper car for the night, he got word that one or two players had brought some beer on board. Sleeper cars back then

---

* Pittsburgh Penguins' Sidney Crosby's injury on January 5, 2011, is remarkably similar. Washington's Mike Green collided with Crosby in the first period of the Winter Classic in Pittsburgh, causing serious head injury to the young superstar.

were the traditional upper- and lower-bunk arrangements, with heavy privacy curtains in each. There were no doors to knock on, so we find George walking through the rolling sleeper car, pulling apart one curtain at a time, up and down, jolting occupants inside – no doubt in various stages of repose – until he exposed two culprits sitting in a top bunk, feet to feet, with their backs comfortably resting against a wall, and a six-pack of beer between the two of them. They had just opened their first beer. "I told them: if we weren't on a moving train, if we were somewhere where we could turn around, or I could put you off the bus – that's what would happen. I took the six-pack of beer and the two opened bottles, walked the length of the sleeper car and over the 'brake'* it went."

After the controversial situation with Lindy Faulkner was finally resolved, the rest of the season continued as a mix of makeshift exhibition games and real contests around the province. Because of the potential demonstrated by this new club from the outset, the NAHA assigned the All-stars to Section "A," the Herder Division in Newfoundland Senior Hockey, while in Section "B" – ironically the more popular of the two and one with regularly scheduled games – a second team represented each community. It relegated any meaningful Section "A" play to take place during the playoffs. Because of this mixture of games, the All-stars unofficial record that year stood at 22-5, and they were more than ready when the playoffs finally began in late April. Meanwhile, the Grand Falls Andcos had made clear their plans to retain the Herder, already demonstrating several times during the year against the All-stars that they were the team to beat.

The best-of-seven 1959 finals would later be described as "the best hockey ever seen in Newfoundland," but would be over in five games. The victorious Grand Falls Andcos would claim their fifth consecutive Herder Memorial Trophy, tying the old St. Bon's record from 1945-49. Games one and two, played in Harbour Grace, were one-goal affairs, the second an overtime win by the Andcos to tie the series at a game apiece. When the series moved to Grand Falls, the goal difference widened substantially, Grand Falls winning games three and four by identical 9-4 scores. In the fifth and final game of the finals, the teams reverted to close hockey once again, with an 8-6 final score.

---

* The "brake" is the small exterior platform of a railway car, overlooking the coupling section.

Unlike the bad-tempered "B" division playoffs between Grand Falls and St. John's the year before (disputes over refereeing and venues had the St. John's team pull out of the series before game seven could be played, forfeiting the title to Grand Falls), there were good feelings all round after this series. The games had been played masterfully and with remarkably good sportsmanship. Alex and George Faulkner, Alfie Hiscock, Brian Wakelin, Sam Gregory, Tom Blackmore, Bucky Hannaford, Ray LaCroix, and both goalies, 'Sham' McInnis and Murray Matheson, played outstanding hockey, game after game. In an unusual gesture seldom seen in sport, fans from Conception Bay made their way into the Grand Falls dressing room after the game, made the rounds of the room, shaking hands with and congratulating each player in turn.

Despite a shortened series, the Division "A" finals clearly showed the calibre of hockey that was possible in Newfoundland, and the kind of interest it had created. NAHA President Vince Rossiter and his officials saw the obvious shift that was coming, and in their executive meetings in April of 1959, began making early preparations for a new set-up in the year ahead: the demise of Division "B" in all-Newfoundland play (to be re-named "Intermediate"), and the controlled expansion* of the senior and more advanced teams in the "A" grouping. Still, it would not be until the 1962-63 season before the NAHA put a firm all-Newfoundland schedule together for regular season play.

In an unexpected and interesting twist of circumstances, the Conception Bay entry in the coming year would be the only club with a roster of "home-grown" Newfoundland players, always an important consideration for the Ceebees' management under George Faulkner.

---

* The NAHA laid down the new rules regarding the number of "professional" players who were allowed to register to play in each community, an open attempt to create a competitive balance among communities. The question of salaried players was an issue not yet on the table.

15

GEORGE, ALEX, AND JACK: 1960

THE 1959 HERDER MEMORIAL TROPHY MIGHT HAVE been in possession of the Grand Falls Andcos, but the year itself belonged to the Conception Bay All-stars, soon to be re-named "Ceebees."* Out of nowhere, it seemed, the team, scrambled together just a few months before and made up of no more than half a dozen experienced players, changed the landscape of hockey in Newfoundland. They would continue to be a formidable presence throughout the next ten years, as fans everywhere filled the arenas to see them. It wasn't just that they were the "new kid on the block" – they had the explosive and exciting Faulkners leading the way.

Adding to their already staggering offence, George and Alex would soon be joined by the youngster of the family, Jack, barely 18 years old, and for the longest while thought to be the least interested in hockey. He'd taken to the game only a few months before, and in just three years time, as a 21-year-old semi-professional with the Johnstown Jets, would find himself among the scoring leaders in his first season in the Eastern Professional League with 31 goals, 40 assists in 70 games. As the Ceebees began looking ahead to the 1959-60 season and another run at the Herder, no one could imagine what effect this newest Faulkner would have on the team and the league. George and Alex, everyone knew, were easily

---

* The name "Ceebees" apparently came from the St. John's *Evening Telegram* sports reporter Max Keeping. The name stuck with the team until their last league appearance in 1969.

the best hockey players in Newfoundland. If young Jack Faulkner came anywhere close in ability, there was no telling where the Ceebees would go next. Even for their established peers in the league, fellows who were well seasoned in the game and playing it close enough to the professional level – the so-called "imports" and semi-professionals – the idea of another Faulkner sharpshooter was still more than intimidating. It was scary.

But for the summer of 1959, his first in Harbour Grace, hockey would take a backseat while George prepared himself for the role of Recreational Director, overseeing softball and soccer competitions – some at the provincial level – and looking ahead to the new stadium's biggest social and commercial event, the Conception Bay Exhibition and Fall Fair. Midge, who had stayed quietly in the background of her husband's hockey world, getting herself established socially and tending full-time to two-year-old Robert, was about to deliver her second child any day in June. Somehow, she had managed to avoid any kind of interruptions during the hockey season – especially during the playoffs. As her time grew nearer, she routinely reminded George to stay close to home: this time, she told him, when her time came, she did not want to have to look for him in someone's basement in some other community.

He remembers removing ice from the stadium floor as the first big task after the hockey season. Some two to three inches of ice had to be removed by hand, loaded into wheelbarrows and carried outside. It was the first time he learned to appreciate what goes on behind the scenes in making a stadium operational. "More to it than just walking into a dressing room, getting dressed for a game, and then going home again right afterwards. It was going to be a busy summer and would take some getting used to in that first year."

The call came on June 19, Father's Day, 1960, at 5 a.m. Midge awoke George with the announcement that she was ready to go. Before reaching the Carbonear hospital, her condition suddenly changed, and she thought it might have been premature of her to make the call. "So, since she was a nurse and knew all the signs, we decided to wait a while before heading to the hospital. Instead, we parked in a place called Crocker's Cove and just sat back and talked, and waited." It seemed only a minute or two later that the baby made its second move, and this time they were off to Carbonear without hesitation.

After Midge was comfortably situated at the hospital, readying for the arrival of their second child, George decided to make his way back home, and hope for more sleep. However, Peter George Vardy Faulkner decided to join the Faulkner family right away with a first cry coming at approximately 7 a.m. He was a light-haired little fellow, recognized immediately as a Faulkner. George was awakened from his brief nap with a call from the hospital staff at Carbonear, telling him, "We have another hockey player over here. He even looks like you."

Despite their commanding presence in NAHA circles, when the hockey season began in November, the Ceebees would not have everything their own way. The new residency rules were in effect, there were more young players making the home teams, and, most importantly, coaching had taken a big step forward in all seven hockey centres that year:

- Buchans, probably the smallest community in the league, had long-time player Bill Scott at the helm and, because of its size, was allowed as many as five mainland players to join the roster.

- Grand Falls had acquired a newcomer – Jean-Paul Pichette – joining veteran coach Joe Byrne. Pichette had been a teammate of George Faulkner's during the Quebec Citadelles season. Pichette would turn out to be one of the best in the league.

- Gander had hired veteran coaching stalwart Wes Trainor on a three-year contract and was expected to be competitive for the first time in years.

- Corner Brook would try to turn its fortunes around under the guidance of coach Orin Carver, another standout in NAHA history.

- Bell Island watched its population grow smaller each year, especially among its hockey elite, as players looked for employment anywhere they could find it. Many settled for the senior league in St. John's; others spread elsewhere throughout the province, leaving veteran George "Scotch" Connors fewer and fewer options in putting a competitive squad together. The loss of a brilliant young goaltender, Bill Sullivan, to Conception Bay, was an especially hard blow to Connors' hopes.

- Although not officially its coach, the presence of Howie Meeker in St. John's – already with two consecutive junior championships to his credit – might finally make a difference there. Jack Vinicombe, an old master of the game from the St. Bon's organization, would officially head the Capitals coaching staff. Like "Scotch" Connors, Vinicombe would soon have his own problems with player recruitment, ironically from the largest player pool in the province.

During the month of February 1961, a few weeks before the official round-robin playoffs would begin, the Ceebees looked like they had a total disaster on their hands. Jimmy Kennedy, George's tough, dependable defence partner, and a team leader in every game, was sidelined for a couple of weeks with injuries, along with George himself, leaving the team's day-to-day roster in critical condition. On February 9, they lost 17-4 to Buchans; two days later they lost to the Miners for a second time, 11-1, an unheard of team defensive lapse of 28 goals in just two games. Their young netminder, Bill Sullivan, felt like he should never have left Bell Island.

During that same disastrous month of February, Faulkner's Ceebees went eight winless games in exhibition play: four losses to Grand Falls and three to Buchans before finally grabbing a tie from the neophyte Gander Flyers. Even the league's top marksman, Alex Faulkner, had suddenly gone silent. To add to their sorrows, word around the league as the playoffs were about to begin was that Buchans, under Bill Scott, were looking like real contenders for the Herder.

Once again, this year the schedule for "A" teams was not released until February when team registration was held. Prior to that time, exhibition games, the fly-by-night arrangement they had endured last year, had teams competing all over the map. Ceebees' Manager Lloyd Andrews was responsible for organizing another round of "tours," starting in Corner Brook and moving east to Grand Falls, Buchans and Gander. These tours entailed hastily arranged scheduling and referee assignments. As far as is known, there was no official recordkeeping. Ticket prices and gate receipts were mutually agreed upon. It was pure exhibition without the frills.

However, one way or another, the teams managed to get in 20 or more games before playoffs, enough to ready them for the Herder competition to come. In the meantime, the "Cinderella" Ceebees had experienced a surprisingly competitive season, and were coming to the realization that winning that first Herder would not be easy, with teams like Buchans and the perennial power-house at Grand Falls about to stand firmly in their way. The Ceebees' weakness, as every team knew, was that beyond the Faulkners, and maybe Jimmy Kennedy, they could be matched player-by-player and line-by-line. There was also the matter of a reduced player roster facing the team. Some games were played with only 11 or 12 players; a third line was often nonexistent, and when it did, it became known in the press as "The Unknown Line," since nobody ever knew for sure who would be on it.

There was also the question of how much longer George Faulkner, though still only 26 years old, could maintain the pace of playing those 60-minute games. The biggest concern, however, was always the prospect of serious injury, especially to mainstream players. If that were to happen, it might mean "kitty-bar-the-door" for the team, and a quick exit from the playoffs.

Jack Faulkner, as he tells it himself, was a hit-and-miss presence with the Ceebees that year, living and studying in St. John's and making the odd weekend trip to Harbour Grace. He'd catch a game here and there, but was never a consistent factor until teammate Neville Pike broke his leg just before the playoffs, and George put even more pressure on him to stay with the team – permanently. "I quit a thousand times. George was a dog. Not that he was a hard task-master – even though he was – but he was as frustrating as hell because he never asked you to do anything on the ice that he wasn't doing himself: stops and starts, shooting, figure eights – all of that. He didn't just ask you to do it, he showed you how to do it. Only a few players had that kind of engine."

Jack had never played in the minor system back home in Bishop's Falls, and he'd never bothered to play at the junior level. His first game was in Senior "A" with the Ceebees, drilled into playing the game in a learning pattern and limiting time-frame the like of which no other player had ever seen. "Thanks to brother George, I learned it all pretty quickly, but it nearly killed me in the process. There were times I thought my arms would fall off from shooting practice, or my legs and hips from skating and more skating practices."

Whatever regimen George used on his kid brother, it worked, and it fell into place at the right time: the 1960 Herder playoffs. After just learning the game of hockey, Jack Faulkner would soon come to love it, and to master it at the same time. And for the time being, the Ceebees had at least one more name they could add to the roster.

The two-division series, East and West, began in March. As expected, Grand Falls came out on top in the 12-game round robin, with nine wins, followed by Buchans, Corner Brook and Gander. In the East, the Ceebees dominated teams from Bell Island and St. John's, winning all eight games, and collecting a record-setting number of points along the way. Alex Faulkner had an amazing 54 points; George – from his defence position – another 35; an unbelievable total of 89 points in eight games. Adding insult to injury it seemed, second-stringers Alfie Hiscock (14-21) and Bill McDonald (8-9) came away with 51 points in that same series. The Bell Islanders* were victims of circumstance, many players leaving the Island to find better employment opportunites in centres that could accommodate them, while at the same time strengthening their own hockey teams. The St. John's players, more than anything, never seemed to be properly organized for the series and were always looking for outside talent. It would take a few more years before they would become competitive against the smaller but more focused centres.

The finals, a best-of-seven affair, would see the first two games played in Grand Falls, home of last year's champions, and the remainder back in Harbour Grace. After the east coast debacle, no one knew what to expect this time round from the Faulkners. How would they and the young Ceebees handle the more powerful and better-balanced Andcos? For one thing, they'd be without the services of Neville Pike, on the sidelines with a broken leg, and an injured Jim Kennedy, who would try to play despite the injury. The team hoped its one replacement, 18-year-old Jack Faulkner, unknown except for the family name, might be able to add some kind of balance. Nevertheless, as the series opened on April 8 and 9 in the papertown, the odds remained heavily in favour of the Grand Falls Andcos.

---

* Each one an All-star, the following players were to leave the Island during those years to play in other communities: Bill Sullivan, Bill McDonald, Bart Ford, Johnny Perry, Mike Fitzpatrick, Gerry Lahey, Dick Power, Mike Kelly, Bern Fitzpatrick, Gordie Butler, Ray Murphy and many others.

While George would continue his 60-minute playing time at the start of the series, he realized that the Andcos would use this strategy against him, "laying back" in the first two periods and coming on with their best efforts in the last, knowing that fatigue had to play a part in Faulkner's performance at that stage. Alex Faulkner, in the meantime, was playing double shifts: being used at centre on the first and third lines. Not an ideal situation facing a team in the finals of a seven-game series. Then there was the question of overtime, which happened in two games, both of which were won by the Andcos. Game one had them winning 5-4 on a goal by Don Smith. Alex managed three of the four goals for the Ceebees in that game, with the injured Jimmy Kennedy scoring the other.

Conception Bay would win Game two by a more comfortable margin of 8-5, on a five-goal performance by young Alfie Hiscock, playing on a line with Alex, who had one goal and four assists. George, still running ahead of the clock, managed two.

Game three, back home in Harbour Grace, was another close affair, with the Ceebees managing an 8-6 victory. This time it was a Bell Islander, Bill McDonald, scoring three goals for the Ceebees. Once again, Alex Faulkner dominated, with two goals and four assists. Even against the powerful Grand Falls Andcos, there was no way of shutting down Alex Faulkner.

Game four began as a romp for the improved Ceebees, who took a three-goal lead only to have the Andcos come back in overtime with winning goals by Don Smith, his third of the game, and "Bucky" Hannaford, with his second. Alex scored two of his team's four goals in that one.

Game five would see the Ceebees take a 3-2 lead in the series, winning another cliffhanger by a score of 4-3.

Game six, the final of that 1960 playoff year, was an unbelievable blow-out for the Ceebees: 16-3. As sometimes happens in games like this, the Andcos had some hard luck in the early part of the game, hitting the goalposts a number of times before the Ceebees' demolition strike got underway. Some say it was the injury to "Bucky" Hannaford in that game which ignited Conception Bay, and perhaps cooled the fervour of the Andcos. It was another night of prodigious scoring statistics: Alex with 6-6, Alfie Hiscock with four goals, and Jack Faulkner with three. George Faulkner, altering his playing style and cutting back the amount of ice time for that game, had two goals and five assists.

For Conception Bay, and its Ceebees, it was their first win of the Herder Memorial Trophy. George Faulkner described the accomplishment as his greatest thrill in sports. The next day's *Evening Telegram* ran a giant headline of just two words on its sports page: THE CEEBEES!!

It had taken them just two years of competition to win the top prize in Newfoundland hockey, the first stage in what would be a decade-long record of continuing successes in NAHA competition.

16

A SECOND CUP

THE THIRD EXHIBITION GAME OF THE 1960-61 NAHA season had the champion Ceebees face off against a St. John's club team, Guards, coached by ex-NHLer Howie Meeker. Strolling through the turnstiles with Meeker that night was his good friend Frank "King" Clancy, assistant GM of the Toronto Maple Leafs that year. The affable Clancy was visiting the city, having just conducted a coaching/refereeing clinic a few days before in Gander. He had a few days to kill, and, at Meeker's invitation, decided to have a look at some local talent while he was here. Among others, the Faulkners would be playing that night at the Prince of Wales Arena, and if last year's performances by these three were any kind of indicators, they were well worth the look.

The season had just started, the players still tuning up for the playoffs a few months away, but you'd never know it from the Ceebees' offensive onslaught in their first two games, scoring a total of 29 goals against the St. John's competition. The Guards had already fallen to the Ceebees at Harbour Grace by a score of 16-2. The game scheduled for December 5 at the arena was just another warm-up, but everyone in the province knew that "King" Clancy was in town, and taking in games whenever he could, and would probably be there.

The two teams played to a full house. No one was expecting anything but a repeat of the outcome of a couple of weeks ago, and that's exactly what they got: Ceebees 13, Guards 3. Alex Faulkner, predictably, gave another outstanding performance, with five goals and four assists. If Clancy was impressed, he never showed it, at least not for the next few days. He left St. John's for a Leafs game in Quebec the next night, with no comment.

Three days later, Thursday of that week, a call came from Ray Myron, a farm-team employee of the Leafs, offering Alex Faulkner a tryout with the Rochester Americans, the Leafs top farm team in the American Hockey League, "King" Clancy had been very impressed. It turned out he wanted both Faulkners. "I don't know if Clancy knew at the time I'd already played professional hockey for four years with the Montreal organization, who still owned my rights as a player, just as the Leafs still held the rights to Howie Meeker, should he ever try to return to the game. He couldn't talk directly to me because of that, so Myron was the go-between, making the offer perfectly legal. In any case, I was just as surprised as anyone else, but I knew where I stood. This was Alex's time. Still, the thought of playing professional hockey together was tempting."

At 24, Alex Faulkner was well past the time of being scouted; that was the purview of much younger hopefuls, 19-year-olds just out of the junior ranks, as George himself had been. Mid-twenties were considered prime years for established NHL players, not a time to be starting out. Alex Faulkner's situation was certainly unique in that era, as it would be today, but it seems Clancy and Meeker had seen something that would override conventional hockey wisdom. From Alex's point of view, age did not matter: the question was whether he could skate and perform with players at that level, or at the AHL level for that matter. Accepting Clancy's offer was one thing, but having to return home, should he not be good enough, was quite another.

George, on the other hand, despite the temptation of wanting to play in the professional ranks with his younger brother, realized how much he would be risking at this stage of his career. The move to Harbour Grace had been a good one for him, as well as his growing family, and he had already established himself as a successful coach and recreation director in the community. The risk was simply not worth it. "I had my chance in professional hockey and I loved it, but right now it was not worth moving on again, as tempting as it was. But I told Alex he had nothing to lose by accepting Toronto's offer. He should definitely have a shot at it."

Alex was pretty sure he could play in the AHL, but there were still things to consider: "These guys were used to playing 70 or more games a year from the time they were in junior. The best we could hope for was maybe 40 or so. I knew the disadvantage there, and it certainly played on my mind." Finally, on Saturday of that week, he made the call to Toronto. He would go, he said, if they would

A SECOND CUP

115

guarantee him a five-game tryout with Rochester. Otherwise, the answer was "not interested." Obviously, Leaf management knew at this early juncture in the season that Faulkner was nowhere near ready to play at the professional level. The Toronto Maple Leafs' coach, the irascible "Punch" Imlach, had decided he wanted to have a look at Faulkner and was ready to concede that the young Newfoundlander needed more conditioning: "You come up to Toronto for a meeting, agree to the move to Rochester, and we'll take it from there. Practice with them for a week, or take as much time as you need, and when you're ready coach Riley* will put you in. You'll have five games to show us what you can do."

Monday morning found Alex skating with the Toronto Marlboros, the Leafs' junior squad. Toronto had played in Detroit on Sunday and had the day off. Alex recalls having a good workout with the Marlboros, going through the usual skating, passing and shooting drills. He remembers how, in the shots-on-goal drill against goalie Bill McNeil "he never stopped one." The practice that morning was followed by a meeting with Imlach – a very cordial one – and Alex was told once again about the arrangements with Rochester. Next day, in a brief workout with the Leafs, Imlach made a point of skating along with Faulkner and telling him, quite frankly, "You can play in the NHL."

To this day, Alex's impressions of his brief stay with the Toronto Maple Leafs' players and staff have never changed: "They were a great bunch to work with, not just as hockey players, but as human beings – very helpful, friendly and encouraging. I never forgot that." After the move to Detroit in 1962, Alex stayed in touch with the Leafs by way of hitching bus rides with the team to see his wife back in Toronto. "I remember when I'd get a chance during a Sunday night game in Detroit, how I'd skate by the Leafs' bench and tell Leafs' trainer Bobby Hackett I needed a ride to Toronto with them on their team bus. 'See me after the game,' he'd say; there was never a problem. When we'd get to Toronto, myself and Bobby would start unloading Leafs' equipment together. Here I am, it's probably five in the morning, and I'm unloading Leafs' hockey gear, and I'm playing with the Detroit Red Wings."

---

* Jack Riley, Rochester Americans coach, 1960-61.

Alex began his playing career, the first of the five games agreed upon, on Christmas Day, 1961. He scored his first goal in his second game as a Rochester American on George's birthday, December 27, at the Colisée in Quebec City. Two days later, December 29, game three, he scored again.

Coach Riley called him into the office after that third game and had him sign on as a professional with the Toronto Maple Leaf organization. He, too, saw a future in the NHL for the blond-haired native of Bishop's Falls.

The Conception Bay Ceebees and the NAHA, at least for the next few years, were a thing of the past.

Alex's loss might have momentarily affected the Ceebees base and certainly put its coach on a new game-planning system. Alex had contributed – by some calculations – more than 60 percent of the team's scoring, and replacing that was going to be difficult, maybe impossible. Looking at his realigned team roster, George still saw strength in the several new faces that had come along: two excellent prospects from Bell Island, Bern Fitzpatrick and Mike Kelly, both destined for exceptional careers in the NAHA. Jack Faulkner, still a dark horse in a way, was now fully committed to the team and about to show real strides in attitude and performance. George liked what he saw in the newcomers and was particularly determined to draw out whatever talents Jack possessed in this new season. He knew Jack could play anywhere, was a good forechecker and strong in the corners. On offence, Brian Wakelin and sharpshooter Alfie Hiscock would return, joining Kelly and Fitzparick in bolstering one of the strongest offensive lineups in the league.

The upcoming province-wide tour – another year of pay-as-you-go exhibition games until the playoffs once again in March – would be a first test of the new lineup. If George had any personal thoughts about playing without Alex for the first time, he kept them to himself. "I think I might have dug inside myself even deeper, and pushed the lads further."

The tour kicked off in early January in Corner Brook, where the Ceebees split a double-header with a much-improved Royals team. They had the same result in a two-game series in Grand Falls. Next, they detoured for a game with Buchans while in the central Newfoundland area, and easily beat the Miners, 7-4. A surprising loss to the Gander Flyers on January 16 in Gander – their second loss to the young Flyers that year – was followed by the first exhibition game in Clarenville against a possible new entry in NAHA competition – the Clarenville Caribous. The game drew a full house, many coming out to see how their new coach and wunderkind, Cy Hoskins, would fare against the powerful Ceebees and George Faulkner. The Caribous went down 11-4, with Hoskins scoring three goals, the last in a one-on-one situation against Faulkner. Hoskins deked Faulkner with a slick move, poking the puck between the veteran defenceman's legs, scoring a spectacular third goal, and delaying the game while a torrent of hats began to hit the ice. The move put the name "Cy Hoskins" on the map. George remembers it well: "He went around me like a hoop on a barrel."

When the playoffs got underway on March 1, the Ceebees were more than ready. Despite the losses incurred during their tour of the island in January, the fences had now been mended and they were about to unleash an unprecedented scoring barrage on all competition. While Corner Brook and Gander were fighting it out for the title out west, the Ceebees were demolishing Bell Island and St. John's in straight games, establishing a scoring record of 36 goals in four games while giving up only ten.

A surprising turn of events had the young upstart Gander Flyers, under a 19-year-old from Cape Breton, Freddie Burke, getting past the more experienced Corner Brook Royals and emerging as the newest challengers to the Ceebees. Despite the buildup, and the exciting play and scoring prowess of young Burke, the Flyers were no match for Faulkner's Ceebees, losing four straight and being outscored by a whopping 50-16.

The NAHA had never experienced such dominance by any one team – a scoring rampage which would probably never be equalled. As the record books show for the 1960-61 playoffs, there were many contributors: young Jack Faulkner, with three "hat-tricks"; Bern Fitzpatrick, with a four-goal effort; Mike Kelly, with a three-and-five-goal display; Alfie Hiscock, with four in one game; and George Faulkner, now a spritely 28-year-old and still playing 60-minute games, with two four-goal games in the eight played that year. It was their second consecutive Herder championship, a remarkable showing that once again had them dancing in the streets in Conception Bay.

17

A ROAD LESS TRAVELLED

FOUR YEARS WOULD PASS BEFORE THE HERDER
Memorial Trophy would once again find its home in Conception Bay. Despite making the playoffs in each of those years following the 1961 victory, the team could not put the finishing touches to the Herder as they once did.

The league was changing. It was one year away from a fully organized, regular schedule, instead of the awkward and confusing exhibition system used until this last year. It would begin as a 16-game format, then move to 20, then 32, and finally to a workable 40-game schedule in 1966. While the exhibition series continued to draw large crowds – often sellouts – the games themselves remained virtually meaningless. There were no points to be gained, no record of ups and downs in team standings, no reference to important things like playoff chances, first-place finishes, or close races – those various factors that make a hockey season what it is. It was not until March 1 of each year, the opening of the playoffs, that hometown fans could look to each game as a serious, meaningful encounter.

As well, teams were getting stronger. Influential community leaders, following the lead of the Moores family in Harbour Grace, began pitching in to attract and sponsor more import players (most still coming from the hockey hotbed on little Cape Breton Island) and the best professional coaches they could find. Sadly, while Bell Island continued to lose its best players, all of them born and bred in the island's fearsome home base of the Monsignor Bartlett Memorial Arena, and Buchans, also struggling to attract exciting lineups, the league would have to look to other centres to maintain the momentum of those earlier years. The once-powerful mining communities, often producing the best and most competitive teams in the province, would soon not be able to compete with the rising economic engines of bigger communities elsewhere. In this new hockey world, economics would rule, and the smaller hockey centres would have trouble keeping up.

The two newest league prospects – Gander and Corner Brook – began to challenge the old NAHA hockey establishment as the 1960s moved on. The Gander Flyers had already shown its beginning strengths in last year's Herder final, even though they had lost the cup in four straight games. They would be back as challengers again this year. Corner Brook would begin its dominance of the league in 1962, when it introduced Frank "Danky" Dorrington.* Under Dorrington's leadership on and off the ice, the Royals would win the Herder Trophy in 1962, 1964, 1966 and 1968. Dorrington would spend 13 years playing in the NAHA, moulding winning teams until the end of the 1968 season, when the hockey tide would finally turn another way. In the case of the competition they would face in 1962, that task would not come easy. In this first year, Dorrington was soon to discover, among other things, that George Faulkner's Ceebees would not be easily intimidated or dismissed. The two teams would establish an historic NAHA rivalry throughout the 1960s, offering exciting NAHA competitions until near the end of the decade.

Almost as a sign of things to come, the first game of the 1962 Herder Finals would be decided in double overtime. It would take a scoring spree of seven goals in the third period to get the Ceebees back in the game, with George Faulkner scoring four and assisting on four others, while younger brother Jack managed four of his own. The reverse happened in the second game. It would be the Royals who would score seven this time – again in the third period, to win 8-2, tying the series at one game each. In the next game the floodgates would open completely, a 15-5 rout by Corner Brook. After trading duplicate scores (8-6) in the next two games, the series ended with a 6-1 win by the Royals, their first Herder championship since 1935.

---

* Recognized by many as the best of the mainland contingent ever to play in the NAHA, Dorrington, born in 1933 in New Glasgow, was inducted into the Newfoundland and Labrador Hockey Hall of Fame in 1996.

Scoring records were again pushed to the limit in this series, with Corner Brook's Doug Hillman finishing up with a total of 19 points in six games; George Faulkner was next with 16 points; and Orin Carver and "Danky" had 15 points each.

The series had been another turkey shoot for the league's biggest stars. The art of goaltending, or defensive hockey as it should be played, had not yet come into its own. Close, low-scoring games happened rarely.

Newfoundland's Senior Hockey League took on its new look for the 1962-63 season, with a 16-game schedule, a return of the St. John's Capitals to the fold, and a one-year hiatus for the Gander Flyers. Bell Island, almost breathing its last, would be gone from the league indefinitely. The Buchans Miners, meanwhile, like the phoenix rising from the ashes, took on new life. With the addition of Neil Amadio and Mike Kelly to their lineup, they would finish atop the league; then, seemingly to everyone's surprise, they would wrap up their first Herder since 1954.

Both semi-final series went the five-game limit: Ceebees lost to Corner Brook, while Buchans eliminated the Andcos. After losing the first two games to the Royals in the best-of-seven final that year, Buchans would win four straight, claiming the championship in six games.

At the end of the 1962-63 season, the first official statistics for the new league set-up looked like this:

TEAMS	GP	W	L	T	PTS
Buchans Miners	16	9	5	2	20
C. Bay Ceebees	16	9	5	2	20
Grand Falls Andcos	16	7	3	6	20
C. Brook Royals	16	6	10	0	12
St. John's Capitals	16	3	11	2	8

SCORING	G	A	PTS
Mike Kelly (Buchans)	28	12	40
Frank Dorrington (C. Brook)	20	16	36
Jack Faulkner (C. Bay)	13	23	36

SCORING	G	A	PTS
Hugh Wadden (Buchans)	20	13	33
Jim Penney (C. Bay)	22	9	31

GOALTENDING	AVE.
Bill Sullivan (Conception Bay)	4.31
Terry Booth (Buchans)	4.50
Mun Pond (Grand Falls)	4.50
Bert Brake (Corner Brook)	5.00
Eg Billard (St. John's)	5.18

HERDER MEMORIAL TROPHY
Buchans Miners

George Faulkner's Ceebees continued their decline in 1964. Finishing fourth in the standings, with just seven wins in 20 games for the season, it was their worst showing by far. The addition of outstanding players, in the persons of Jimmy Dawe, Al Dwyer and Bell Island's young Gerry Lahey, gave a bright outlook for the new year, despite the loss of Jack Faulkner to the professional ranks with the Johnstown Jets.

The team's 12 losses came mostly at the hands of the Corner Brook Royals and Buchans Miners, while the lowly Gander Flyers were their victims in their four meetings for the year. The team's goals-against average was second highest in the league, just ahead of Gander. It was an unusual and certainly painful comedown.

The humiliation continued in their semi-final playoff series against the tenacious Buchans Miners. They were throttled in five games by the Miners, allowing 55 goals against. In one particular game, Buchans' big forward from Nova Scotia, Hugh "Red" Wadden, a star performer year after year, found himself going one-on-one against George, and with a surprisingly sudden move, beat Faulkner cleanly: "I think I must have been too far out near the blueline when I saw "Big Red" sweeping in over centre and then heading right for me – a full head of steam going for him. I lined him up and thought I had him, when he suddenly did a spin-a-rama* on me, goes around like I'm standing still and then hits the post with a great shot. We both laughed a lot over the years after that one."

Meanwhile, the series between the Corner Brook Royals and the St. John's Capitals had gotten underway in St. John's, with the Capitals winning the first two games at home. A planned flight to Corner Brook for Friday night's encounter at Humber Gardens was waylaid when the aircraft experienced mechanical problems in Gander. A new starting time of 10:30 p.m. instead of the original 8:00 p.m. was set, assuming the St. John's team could make alternate plans using another aircraft. The story then gets muddy. Each side took a different position as to why the Capitals never did make it on time, and the game was cancelled outright. Everyone expected it would simply be rescheduled. Instead, the provincial executive, in an act of unprecedented stupidity, awarded it to the Royals by default because the St. John's team was a "no show."

The executive spent the entire weekend trying to resolve the matter, while allowing the teams to continue the series on Saturday night, a game won by Corner Brook. When St. John's requested to replay the cancelled game on Sunday afternoon, and was finally and officially turned down, the team decided they had had enough of the nonsense and flew home, forfeiting the series to Corner Brook – a disturbing set of circumstances that paved the way for Corner Brook's second win of the Herder Trophy in three years.

To no one's surprise, the following season, 1964-65, did not include a team from St. John's. Perhaps even more surprising that year was the return of the undaunted, ever-popular Bell Island Islanders back to the league.

---

* The word 'spin-a-rama' was first coined in the 1970s by Montreal Canadiens' broadcaster Danny Gallivan when describing a move made famous by their all-star defenceman Serge Savard. Savard would seem to make a move in one direction and then quickly spin right around in the opposite, leaving the opposing defenceman just standing there.

18

GEORGE, ALEX, AND JACK: 1965

ALEX FAULKNER'S BRIEF NHL CAREER BEGAN AT AGE 25 in 1962 and ended at the end of the 1963-64 season. The league was just a few years from its historic expansion plans beginning in 1967 when it would double in size, going from "the original six" to 12 teams. Sid Abel, Detroit Red Wings' coach in 1964, would only offer Alex a place with the AHL's Pittsburgh Hornets for the next season, a loss of both prestige and money for the young Newfoundland player. "I told Sid I would only stay if they kept my salary at the NHL level. After all, I knew I could make as much back home with the Ceebees as I could in Pittsburgh."

Whether he realized it or not, the two-year stint back home would be a disadvantage when the time came for the expansion draft in two years time. "I don't know if it mattered or not. In my last year in Rochester, I was the top scorer with the club, received the team's Offensive Player Award, and so on, and yet six or seven guys on that team who were well below me in the scoring were drafted into the NHL. Maybe I should've played in Pittsburgh that year after all." The injuries he had incurred with the Red Wings in that second year – a battered wrist and torn ankle ligaments – could not have helped in his overall assessment at the time: he'd played in less than half the team's games, and his conditioning was becoming an important factor they would certainly have considered. As he was nearing his 30th birthday, age also may have been in the mix. In any event, the decision was made and he would be back home in Conception Bay for the 1964-66 seasons.

In the meantime, in that same springtime of 1964, Jack Faulkner was finishing up an impressive year in the Eastern Hockey League (EHL) with the

Johnstown Jets, playing 70 games, with 31 goals and 71 points, placing him fourth overall in team scoring. He, too, would be returning to the Conception Bay Ceebees but for a different reason: Detroit bypassed him when inviting tryouts to their camp that year. Despite the numbers which the youngest Faulkner had shown in his first year in the pros, he was overlooked when contacts were made for the tryouts with Detroit, and didn't know what to make of it: "I couldn't figure out why they left me out. I was young, I'd had a reasonably good first year, and I was expecting to go back. But I guess it was not to be."

All of which spelled good fortune for George Faulkner. The trio would be reunited and, true to form, would make the Ceebees strong challengers once again for the Herder. In addition, George had come across some pretty exciting players looking to break into his already powerful lineup for the 1964-65 season. Among them was a colourful St. John's native, 22-year-old Hubert Hutton. "Hutton was one of two or three guys from the city – Wally McDonald and Adrian Smith were the others – who'd often come out to Harbour Grace to practice with us, and we got to know them. Hubert was particularly impressive and we knew he wanted to play, so we signed him for that year." George recalls Hutton's playing style: "He was a wonderful skater – should've been a figure skater maybe – and had a great shot. I used to think he never took the game seriously enough. He was quite the character, great for team spirit." As well as a strong skating style, Hutton's trademark was a booming slapshot. According to teammates, the shot was often deflected and just took off in any direction, usually upward. In games played at the St. John's Memorial Stadium, the victim was often a sizable picture of the Queen, hanging over the north end of the rink. "Bad enough that he could shoot with such strength, but to see Hubert set up with a rolling puck coming at him was a frightening sight altogether."

Hutton would compete for nearly two decades in NAHA competition, mostly with St. John's Capitals. In overall point totals, he finished his career second only to George Faulkner in scoring for defencemen, with 106 goals and 254 points.

At 18, Gerry Lahey was tearing the Bell Island senior league apart, at one point scoring 29 goals in a three-game championship series. He was making headlines in the local hockey world and finally came to the attention of George Faulkner and the Ceebees. "I heard about this kid and his incredible scoring punch, so I called him and asked if he was interested in working and playing in Harbour Grace. He came over and as soon as his skates hit the ice I could see that he was a hockey player: he looked and skated like a hockey player. Lahey was a dipsy-doodler,* could stickhandle, deke, fake and had all the moves." George set him up on a line with Alex and Jack that year and the trio led the league in points scored. In an incredible NAHA legacy of 257 games played, Gerry Lahey would leave behind a scoring record of 232 goals and 437 points.

Bishop's Falls native Harold Stanley was another standout. He was, as George put it, "the best of the defensive defencemen." Not a big player, not a great scorer, and not very heavy, but a strong skater who could hit like no other." Stanley was another one of those Bishop's Falls lads with no minor hockey experience who learned the game on the river and on the ponds nearby. He grew up during the years when George himself was playing in Quebec, so the contact came from Alex, who was always impressed with Stanley's potential. In a poll taken shortly after his retirement, Harold Stanley was voted one of the top ten players ever to play in Newfoundland. His best years would be spent playing with the Faulkners in Conception Bay, and later representing Grand Falls in Allan Cup play. His first year with the Ceebees, 1964-65, would mark the beginning of all that.

Despite their immense firepower, the Ceebees would not easily shake off the Corner Brook Royals throughout the regular season. While they would finish in first place, with 17 wins and 35 points, the Royals weren't far behind, with 16 wins, 1 tie, and 33 points. At playoff time, the anticipation of seeing these two teams meet once again for the Herder – especially with the three Faulkners back – was at an all-time high. Extra seating and sleeper cars were added at Canadian National Railways to handle the increased passenger traffic between Conception Bay, Grand Falls and Corner Brook. A call to CN the day before would detail how many fans were expected on this or that playoff date, how many sleeper cars would be needed and how much on-board service the company would need to prepare for.

126

----

* The term 'dipsy-doodler' probably goes back to the NHL's Bentley brothers, Max and Doug, in the late 1940s and early 1950s. It was a showy style of play, full of neat stickhandling displays mixed with fancy and unexpected skating moves that delighted hockey fans every time.

Another kind of "sleeper" in this series would turn out to be the Buchans Miners themselves, third-place finishers during the regular season, with only nine wins and 20 points, but about to put on an exciting hockey display that would almost preempt the interest level of the finals itself. Hector Caines, Mort Verbiski, Frank Finlayson, Billy Malone, Don Barrett and Hugh "Red" Wadden were not about to go down quickly or easily. The Corner Brook Royals, still fresh from a four-game sweep of the Grand Falls Andcos in the other series, could only stand by and watch as the semi-finals between the Miners and the Ceebees continued.

In regular season play, the Ceebees had easily swept four games each from Bell Island, Grand Falls and Gander, but had some trouble against Corner Brook, with two wins, one tie and a loss. They managed easy wins against Buchans in their first two encounters, but ran into a more determined squad in the second set. They won each game by a close score, and it was a tough, competitive encounter each time. The first two games of the playoffs would open in Buchans, and the Ceebees found themselves facing a much better and much more determined team. Typical of the Conception Bay squad, they would go into this series with a limited roster, usually no more than 13 players, sometimes as few as 11. But their conditioning, always a big factor in George Faulkner's coaching philosophy, would help fill the player void. Buchans, meanwhile, would ice a full squad and were looking to standby goaltender Mark Leyte to be at his best. Leyte had served as backup goalie with the team for six years. The 1965 semi-finals would be his chance to finally get himself established. If he could stop the Faulkners and Gerry Lahey, he would come out of the series as some kind of hero – to the enthusiastic fans of the small town of Buchans, a very real one.

Both games were close. In game one, the Miners came away with a close 7-5 victory, avenging their losses to Conception Bay during the regular season, but fell 8-5 in game two, with Jack Faulkner adding three more goals to the pair he tallied in game one.

The series shifted back to Harbour Grace for game three – a Monday night contest – and it would see a haggard Buchans crew take to the ice, after living through a 15-hour bus trip over some very difficult roads. The trip normally took nine hours – enough of a trial without the added six. The Miners took a terrible 12-3 shellacking, with Alex and George getting ten points between them and Gerry Lahey contributing one goal and five assists for the night. The series looked as if it might be all over.

At first, game four began to look like a slug-fest. The teams traded goals for the first 50 minutes, and then turned it into an exciting cliffhanger. The score stood at 9-9 in the third period, until Buchans, led by Finlayson and Barrett once again, finally opened it up with three unanswered goals. The final score: Buchans 12, Ceebees 10. Newspaper reports the next day had the Miners outskating and outhustling the Ceebees, shorthanded again with the usual three defencemen and two forward lines. The series was now tied at two games each.

Someone described game five as "probably the best game ever played in the Harbour Grace Stadium." It would certainly be the biggest testing ground yet for Buchans' goalie Mark Leyte. The young netminder kept the Miners in the game for the first two periods and wound up handling 50 shots over the 60 minutes, against a mere 25 for Terry Matthews of the Ceebees. The Ceebees, despite a manpower shortage once again, came up with five goals in the third period, finally winning 7-5. The feeling was, on both benches, that neither team could play any better than they just had. It was a great night for Conception Bay hockey fans and a bittersweet loss for the Buchans Miners.

The series ended with a 6-1 Ceebees' victory in game six. Buchans' Neil Amadio later commented that his team played their hearts out but, in close games, couldn't get the big goal when they needed one. George Faulkner put the series win down to his team's conditioning. For "the dog," as his brother Jack had described him earlier, it was always conditioning. From the moment he had taken over the team, before the first game was ever played, he insisted on hard work and conditioning at every turn. At playoff time, and in a close series such as the one the Ceebees and Miners had just been through, he knew conditioning might always determine the outcome.

In a newspaper interview during these playoffs, Alex Faulkner described the difficulty he was having in adjusting to the style and pace of play in the NAHA. The slow speed of the game, of course, wasn't the only problem, but more than that, he wasn't always able to do things with the same skill and finesse he was used to in the pro leagues. For anyone who has ever had to play at a lower level of the game, it made sense: it is frustrating not to be able to finish off plays, to give and receive passes at a slower pace, and to have to stickhandle your way most of the time. "The mind-set is to want things to go faster, with team play, but it's more of an individual's game in this league," Alex said. "In the pro set-up it's always a team effort, and everyone is on the same level with the same expectations. Everything's more predictable."

Just a few days after that interview, Alex claimed the league scoring title, tallying one goal and eight assists in the last game of the season, moving past Corner Brook's "Danky" Dorrington. Dorrington had a three-point lead going into the last game of the season.*

The Corner Brook Royals first began to establish themselves as NAHA perennial challengers with their meeting against the Ceebees back in 1962, winning their second Herder Memorial Trophy that year. The year marked the beginning of a consistent run of championships or runner-up finishes that would continue until this year, when they would line up once again against the Conception Bay Ceebees.

The opening game of the 1965 finals had all the appearances of the Royals looking to make another convincing run at the Herder. They squeaked by the Ceebees 7-6. On the winning goal the puck bounced off George Faulkner's skate and rolled past a shocked Terry Matthews. At one point in that game, the Royals had three men in the penalty box, opening up two breakaways for sharp-shooting Gerry Lahey. Lahey missed both, hitting the goal post each time.

But that would be all for the Royals. They went on to lose the finals four straight. With the exception of a 12-5 rout in the final game at Harbour Grace, however, they stayed competitive in each of the others. Game three had the two teams even for some 58 minutes, until Lahey and Jack Faulkner put the game away with goals for the Ceebees.

Conception Bay continued to play the finals shorthanded, with Jim Penney injured, and St. John's native Hubert Hutton barred from further play after game one. The Royals protested that he was ineligible to play under the league's residency rule. In fact, the winning Ceebees' team picture, which appeared in the local papers at the end of that final, showed only eleven men dressed for the final game. It was another one of those "conditioning" miracles for which they were becoming so well known.

---

* Jack Faulkner would lead all goal scorers that year with 33 goals in 20 games.

Unofficial scoring records for the entire 1965 playoffs show the Faulkners with 89 points, while Gerry Lahey alone would contribute another 36. It would be the last appearance together for the high-flying Faulkner brothers and the Ceebees' spectacular foursome.

Ironically, circumstances in the next season would change the team's fortunes dramatically, leaving 1965 as the high point in the history of the team. While the next few years would see them add one more Herder to their accomplishments (1967), the demise of the once-powerful Conception Bay Ceebees was slowly about to happen.

1966

PART FOUR

WORLD ICE HOCKEY
CHAMPIONSHIPS: TEAM CANADA

1966

19

"WHO'S FATHER BAUER?"

*I remember it was the camp director, Rollie McLenahan, who first approached me.
I think it was right after our first game in camp that week. He told me Father Bauer
wanted to talk to me. I asked, "Who's Father Bauer?" That'll tell you how naïve
I was at the time. Anyway, I met him later that day and he asked me – right out:
"Would you like to play for Canada?" I never even blinked. "Yes," was all I said.*

IT WAS AUGUST, 1965, DURING A CANADIAN AMATEUR
Hockey Association (CAHA) Coaches' Minor Hockey Clinic in St. Andrews,
New Brunswick, and George Faulkner had just been invited by Father David
Bauer to join Canada's national team at the World Ice Hockey Tournament in
March 1966, in Ljubljana, Yugoslavia.

His first reaction to Father Bauer's invitation was to wonder: at age 34,
why me? Of the dozen or so players from home attending the camp that week,
George's feeling was that most of them were quite capable of making the national
squad as well, and many were much younger. He knew the emphasis in this
new program was based on youth, Father Bauer's long-term development
system whereby players could spend several years growing with the team while
still pursuing a university education. "I was so thrilled to be asked, I never did
bring up the subject of age. I guess what they saw, they liked." It reminded him
of the kind of responsibility he had undertaken back in 1951 or so, when he was
the first Newfoundlander to move on to the professional ranks. Expectations
were pretty high back then, and he didn't disappoint. Here he was again, at 34,
about to accept the same kind of role, but he wasn't a kid anymore.

Father David Bauer, a Catholic priest from the Congregation of St. Basil, and a native of Kitchener, Ontario, had become one of the biggest names in Canadian hockey circles, as creator of a national hockey program to re-establish Canada's position in world hockey. Senior "amateur" clubs and Allan Cup champions like the Trail Smoke Eaters, perennial contenders in the early 1960s, seemed no longer able to compete successfully at that level. While other countries could bring out their very best players to participate in the annual event, the International Ice Hockey Federation (IIHF) did not yet permit professional or semi-professional players, such as Canada's best in the NHL, to compete. European players, no matter what their abilities, were all classified under "amateur" status.

It was Bauer's idea to change the status of Canadian players by putting together a permanent hockey program to offset the decline in competition. He put forth the idea of establishing a national team made up mostly of university players, together with a spattering of the best of non-professional senior league players from across the country. The CAHA, with practically no other choice, agreed with the plan and the program got underway immediately. The university group was funded entirely by the CAHA and was to be administered by a group headed by Father Bauer. By 1965, when George Faulkner came along, the program was well established and Canada was once again competing internationally at a very successful level. However, it was the Soviet Union which still dominated the international tournaments, winning the competition that year for the third straight time. Canada had last won the cup in 1961.

David Bauer was born into a well-known hockey family. Older brothers Frank and Bobby had played in the NHL, the latter a Hockey Hall of Fame inductee, and a member of Boston's famous "Kraut Line" back in the 1940s. Father Bauer is remembered as an inspirational leader as well as a hockey authority. He believed in teaching the fundamentals of the game: skating, passing, stick-handling, and shooting. He saw the game as more than just building athletic skills: he wanted to instill character into his players – moral conditioning, as he described it – as he went along. The opportunity was there for young, capable athletes to combine education with hockey training, a unique kind of vision which, as time went on, would prove itself successful in both disciplines.

As usual, Midge Faulkner was all for the idea. She remained the Ceebees' biggest and loudest fan, never missing a game year after year, and as enthusiastic about hockey and watching George play as when they first met back in Shawinigan years before. As well, her love for the team knew no bounds. Her favourite spot at home games was behind the team's bench, where she could more easily rally the troops after each line change, or each magical play or highlight. Typical of the kind of spirit she showed and the fun she could have were the taunts she'd make at the team's young star, Alex Faulkner. Even when he would be at his peak in scoring, and coming off the ice with "just another goal" or another hat trick, Midge would be standing over him, chiding away: "What are you doing, coming off so soon? Are you getting too old for this game already? Get back out there!" She wore a heavy fur coat, her trademark at each game. Despite the frigid arena temperatures in those days, she wore the coat open, excited or overheated with all that jumping around and screaming for her favourite Ceebees.

There was never a question of holding him back from anything remotely connected to the game of hockey. The hard part was that she was not sure she could attend the camps with him, to share in all the excitement of travel and watch him play again all across the country. As things would pan out, she would soon get a measure of both, in circumstances much more memorable and adventurous than she or anyone else could have imagined.

The one issue remaining before a final decision could be made was that of George's salary. Who would pay the bills while George would be taking a half-year's leave from his positions with the Ceebees and the Harbour Grace Stadium? When board chairman Frank Moores was told of the chance to play, his reaction was no surprise: "George, you gotta go for it." The local member of government at that time, Claude Sheppard, took the matter directly to Newfoundland Premier J.R. "Joey" Smallwood. Without hesitation, Smallwood invested sufficient funds with the Harbour Grace organization to cover George's salary for the 1965-66 operations. In the meantime, Alex Faulkner agreed to coach the Ceebees in George's absence. The deal was set.

Midge was delighted with the prospect of moving to Winnipeg. The change was a welcome one after living seven years in the small community of Harbour Grace, and it would mean an opportunity for family travel to other parts of the country, or so she thought. For George, the past summer had been a longer than usual layoff, and he felt he needed more time than ever to get in shape. "By the time I had all the personal arrangements in place in late October – renting my new home in Harbour Grace and finding one for my family in Winnipeg, plus getting the boys started in a new school – the training camp in Winnipeg had ended. I'd missed the whole thing. I had no other choice when I arrived than to go to the arena, put on my gear, and get on with it." Not the best way to prepare for a tournament of any kind, let alone this one.

It turned out that there would be plenty of time ahead to get in shape for Europe. Canada's National Team (the "Nats") had made its home base in Winnipeg for the first time in 1965, away from Vancouver, their home since 1962. The commitment by players was for a six-month period: October to March, 1966. The schedule – practices and exhibition games across the hockey map of western and central Canada (they did not play east of Quebec, and NHL teams were off limits, for some reason) – was nearly overwhelming. They visited every major centre, with games against teams from the AHL, WHL, and western senior teams. Exhibition matches against the Soviets, Czechs and Swedes were held in Victoria, Edmonton, Lethbridge, Kimberley and London, with the team flying back home to its base in Winnipeg after each game.

By the time December rolled around, they were getting ready for a trip to the U.S.A., where they would compete in a Christmas/New Year's tournament in Denver, Colorado. George's guitar playing and love for frequent, old-fashioned sing-a-longs was becoming popular with the team, especially at this time of year, so much so that they collected enough money to buy a new guitar for their nightly sessions. "It was an old black guitar, and not a very good one," he remembered, "but it had six strings on it." The team finished the tournament with a silver medal, losing once again to the Soviets. No sooner had they arrived back home in Winnipeg and resumed practices when one of their players, John Russell, suffered a severe eye injury and had to leave the team permanently. The incident left a considerable strain on team morale, just as the team was preparing to go overseas.

The team's training schedule would finish with a series of exhibition matches in Europe before the start of the World Tournament in the first week of March. By the time they reached Europe for their final round of warm-up exhibition games, and not a particularly successful run, the team lineup was very much set: they would go with three goalies, three pairs of defence and thirteen forwards. Their first game was played at the RCAF base in Baden-Baden, Germany, where playing-coach Jackie McLeod led the team with four goals. The Nats beat the Air Force squad easily, 14-2. A second serious injury occurred to a team member in that game in Germany. Like John Russell, Rick McCann had been playing forward, leaving the team again shorthanded up front and necessitating a quick change in plans for George Faulkner's role. McLeod decided to resurrect Faulkner's playing skills at left wing, even though, as George explained, "I hadn't played up front for nearly ten years." Another adjustment for the team's second-oldest player, at 34, but one which would prove to be a sign of good things to come.

The team would go on to win only one more of the five exhibition games played, a comfortable 7-1 victory against lowly Yugoslavia. Losses to the Czechs (4-0, 4-2) and to the improving U.S.A. squad (2-1) closed out the dismal exhibition round. It placed them in the position of being uncertain finishers in the tournament about to get underway. However, the team's three goalies – Wayne Stephenson, Seth Martin and Ken Broderick – were improving with every game and getting an equal share of ice time. The young Canadian team, with an average age of just 22, had done whatever was asked since its coming together in October past, and was now ready to perform – despite some harsh setbacks – beyond anyone's expectations.

Jackie McLeod had been a member of Canada's last gold medal world championship team in 1961. He was the leading scorer that year for the Trail Smoke Eaters. The Soviet Union had taken over ever since, seeming to get stronger each time. There was little doubt in McLeod's mind that the Canadians had quite a challenge on their hands. They felt comfortable enough taking on the Swedes and Czechs, although the Czechs were up and coming on the world stage as well. McLeod, now the oldest member of the team at 36, remained a constant scoring threat on his own, but more than that, he knew the Soviet style as well as anyone could, giving the Nats a little advantage as the tournament began.

The players were billeted at a three-storey residence in downtown Ljubljana, overlooking an elementary school courtyard. In their leisure time, whenever a group of them gathered on the balconies, the young school kids could be seen looking up at them, waving from the school windows below. A few of the players used such moments to have some fun with the kids – dropping colored

1960 CONCEPTION BAY CEEBEES FIRST HERDER MEMORIAL CHAMPIONSHIP. A. Crocker, J. Kennedy, G. Faulkner, F. Fleming, J. Coady, J. Penney, A. Dawe, J. Faulkner, C. Penney, L. Andrews, (seated) E. Pumphrey, J. Thomey, B. McDonald, F. Rossiter, A. Hiscock, A. Faulkner, B. Sullivan

GEORGE CHASES A ROLLING PUCK against Valleyfield Braves goalie Andrew Payette.

"THE COBRA," CEEBEES BRILLIANT GARY SIMMONS, makes the save against St. John's Capitals Ian Campbell. George Faulkner looks on.

1961 ROCHESTER AMERICANS, TORONTO MAPLE LEAFS FARM TEAM. Alex Faulkner (seated, third left) would go on to play just one game with the Leafs. All but three players in the photo would play in the NHL.

CEEBEES DUO – GEORGE AND ALEX. The two would dominate the NAHA throughout the 1960s.

LEAVING FOR THE WORLD CHAMPIONSHIPS, OCTOBER 1965. Left to right: Claude Sheppard (MHA for Harbour Grace), George, Jack, Robert, Midge and Peter.

CANADA'S PLAYING COACH, JACKIE MCLEOD speaks with George during a team practice in Winnipeg. McLeod was leading scorer with the gold-winning Canadian team in 1961, and selected for the tournament's all-stars.

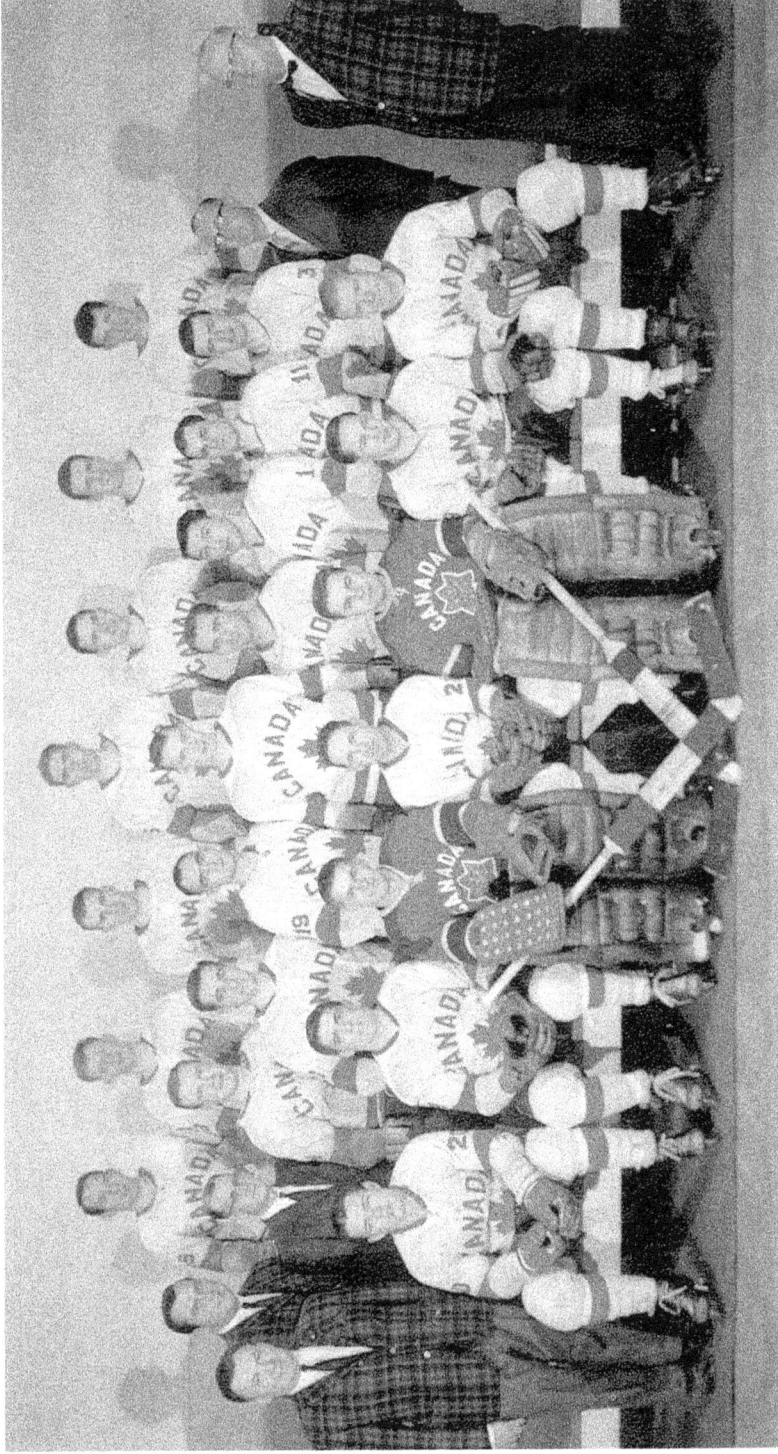

CANADA'S NATIONAL HOCKEY TEAM 1965-66. Left to right: (front row) Bill Bozak, Morris Mott, Roger Bourbonnais, Wayne Stephenson, Jack McLeod, Henry Goy, Fran Huck, George Faulkner, Jack Waugh. (middle row) Phil Reimer, Charlie Maddin, Barry MacKenzie, Al McLean, Harvey Schmidt, John Russei, Ray Cadieux, Duane McPhail, Ted Hargreaves, Paul Conlin, Reid Taylor. (back row) Rick McCann, Jean Cusson, Marshall Johnston, Wayne Mosdell, Gary Begg, Terry O' Mallory, Billy MacMillan. (missing) Gary Dineen, Ken Broderick, Lorne Davis, Father David Bauer.

JACK AND ALEX. As well as time spent playing in NAHA competition, the two would play professionally in the 1960s: Alex with Toronto Maple Leafs, Detroit Red Wings, Rochester Americans and San Diego Gulls, and Jack with the Johnstown Jets.

postcards of team pictures onto the courtyard. The fluttering postcards caused a small stampede every time. George recalls, "It wasn't long before the same kids who'd been in the windows were out in the courtyard, picking up the postcards and then running back inside. After a while, I think even a few of the teachers got in on the act." Canadian souvenirs falling from the sky.

The world tournament opened for Canada on Wednesday, March 2, and their first outing,* against the U.S.A., could not have gone better, both for Jackie McLeod as coach, and George Faulkner as the new left winger. The Nationals had an easy 7-2 win, with George getting two unassisted goals from his new position. McLeod would still use him on defence when necessary, and he was used pretty much as a regular on the power play. Of the remaining teams they would face in the early going, it was the East Germans they feared most. They had surprised the favoured Swedes 4-1 earlier, the biggest tournament upset so far.

The schedule had them play back-to-back weekend games against Finland and Poland. Both were relatively easy wins: 9-1 against Finland and a 6-0 shutout over Poland. Both George and a young spitfire centre from Regina, Saskatchewan, 21-year-old Fran Huck, had two goals and an assist. Goalie Ken Broderick registered his first of two consecutive shutouts in the game.

Despite the early pressure that was mounting as they approached the game with East Germany the following Tuesday, the Nationals won handily, 6-0, although newspaper reports, and comments from the players themselves, described it as their weakest effort so far. Nevertheless, it was the team's fourth win, tying them for the moment at the top of the standings with Russia and Czechoslovakia. Canada's goaltending record was equally impressive: allowing only three goals in four starts. However, the real test was coming: Czechoslovakia on Thursday, Russia on Friday, and the final against Sweden on Sunday. The game against the Czechs would be the most memorable of them all, raising a disturbing and perennial problem for Canadian hockey teams playing in Europe: European referees.

---

* The biggest opening-day crowd, ten thousand strong, took in the game between Canada and the U.S.A., Yugoslavia's president, Marshall Tito, among them. Surprisingly, the Russia/Czechoslovakia game that same day drew only half that number. George pointed out that the other surprise Yugoslavia had for them was when members of the team had to forfeit their passports while in the country.

Czechoslovakia, like the Russians, used their best players in all world tournaments, and was slowly closing parity with Canada's best – players of NHL calibre. Jackie McLeod and the rest of his coaching staff paid full respect to the Czech team, but recognized that they were not the power that Russia was, and that, in any given tournament or game, they were beatable. The Denver, Colorado, tournament in January had shown that. Still, in pre-tournament games just completed in Europe, Canada had lost both games to the skillful Czechs. As they stood ready for the opening faceoff at the World Tournament game in 1966, both teams knew what was possible. Sadly, as newspaper headlines showed the next day, the game was marred by questionable refereeing and almost resulted in the Canadian team packing their bags and heading home.

A goal by Czechoslovakia's great Jiri Holik in the first period held up until midway through the third, when Roger Bourbonnais of Canada, "on a beautiful pass" from George Faulkner, tied it at 1-1. Up to this point in the game, the Canadians had suffered a string of penalties and a disallowed goal by Ray Cadieux in the second period, when the Czech goalie, Vlado Dzurilla, and one of his defencemen knocked the net off its moorings. "The puck was already about a foot over the line," according to defenceman Lorne Davis. Later, in the third period, another disallowed goal – this one by Faulkner. The play was called down over an isolated call by the Polish referee, Andrei Chojnacki. The *Montreal Gazette* described it this way: "(Marshall) Johnson's stick got entangled in a Czech player's skate. Johnson let go of his stick, but the Czech fell anyway. Chojnacki whistled Johnson down just before Faulkner's shot beat Dzurilla."

Holik's earlier goal had caused another stir on the Canadian bench, and for very good reasons. The same referee had called a double minor against team captain Terry O'Malley and *wanted to put two men off*, until McLeod stood his ground and explained the rules rather forcefully. "When I wouldn't let him do that, he gave Marshall Johnson a minor a few seconds later. *After the Czechs scored, he was going to keep both men in the penalty box. It was only after much protesting that he let one out.*"*

---

* From Canadian Press reporter Carl Mollins' article, appearing in the *Evening Telegram*, March 12, 1966.

It only got worse for the Nationals. With just 28 seconds left in the game, score still tied, Czech forward Stanislav Pryl, who had set up Holik's goal earlier, put the game away with a picture goal against Seth Martin at 19:32. It was Canada's first loss of the tournament. The dressing room scene that followed was just as frustrating and dramatic as what had just transpired on the ice.

"It's time we quit the farce and played our own hockey," Jackie McLeod fumed in the dressing room. The Canadians, almost unanimously, had just elected to quit the tournament and go home. It became a lengthy and boisterous meeting, most players wanting to chuck it all in. They counted up the penalty calls during the game: eleven against Canada and four against the Czechs. Hardly a balanced effort, as they saw it, and a blatant continuance of poor officiating at earlier tournaments and games. Despite having to adjust to the larger ice surface in European arenas, and a number of different rules for the European game, and incompetent – perhaps biased – refereeing, Canadian teams were expected to put up with all of it. Protesting, as Father Bauer commented after the game, was useless: "What good would it do?"

A second team meeting was called immediately, this time with Bauer, Lionel Fleury, president of the CAHA, and Gordon Jukes, secretary-manager of the same organization, sitting in. Maybe it was fatigue finally setting in, or simply that they began to see the full import of what quitting might mean, but the tone of this second meeting had softened somewhat, and after a few minutes they decided, to a man, to play out the tournament. But there was no mistaking why they changed their minds: "We did it for Father Dave," was the way one player put it.

Goalie Seth Martin, named to the tournament's first all-star team along with defenceman Gary Begg and centre Fran Huck, put it bluntly: "One would get the impression it was a fix." Many others thought the same thing.

In fact, as George remembered, a reporter for the *Toronto Star*, a Czech-born Canadian, George Grosse, came into their dressing room at some point and confirmed the story. "Grosse said he overheard a conversation between the referees and the management of the tournament, basically saying that there was no way the Canadians were going to win that game."

Of all that had transpired that evening the worst effect had to be exhaustion. They had just played three intense and frustrating periods of hockey, controlling a pent-up bitterness throughout, losing in the final seconds, and then sitting through two nerve-racking meetings on whether to continue with the tournament. In the back of their minds there had to be the pressing thought of having to face a formidable Russian team in just a few hours' time.

On this, the biggest day of the tournament, things could not have gone worse for the young Canadian squad.

Friday, March 11, came quickly. A sell-out crowd of twelve thousand was on hand to watch the most anticipated game of the tournament: Canada vs. Russia. Despite the fatigue, and misgivings in the minds of several players, the Canadians proved they were ready. It would be the hardest-fought game of the series, and only in the later minutes of the third period did any kind of fatigue begin to show. Forechecking became the key to the Canadian game, and there was little doubt that the Russsians knew what was coming. Before scoring their first of three goals late in the first period, the Russians became embroiled in a bench-clearing incident with the Canadians when Canada's Lorne Davis, a 5'10" defenceman, tangled with Russia's Aleksandr Ragulin, 6'1", 218 pounds, along the boards. For the Russians, the message was clear: this game would be their toughest.

The 1-0 score held until the five-minute mark of the third period when the Russian "machine" finally began to take over, with two quick goals. Seth Martin remembers the speed they could muster all of a sudden, and the quickness of their passing and shooting. Although losing by a final score of 3-0, the Nationals came away with a feeling of great pride, and the mood at the end of that game in no way resembled what had happened with the Czechs. "The Russians are a great hockey team," said Father Bauer after the game. Marshall Johnson added, "It was no disgrace to lose to a team like that."

Still, the loss was a heavy-hearted one for Canada. With the score still at 1-0, playing-coach Jackie McLeod had hit the post, followed by a breakaway when Gary Begg fired the puck into the goalie's pads.

After all the dressing room chatter, George managed to put a positive spin on it all: "Don't think we didn't have the Russians worried!"

All that was left for Canada was the final game, played Sunday afternoon, March 12 – the bronze medal game against the Swedes. Again, the Canadian squad showed their character, coming from behind, a 1-0 deficit, and beating the Swedes 4-2, finishing in third place behind Russia and Czechoslovakia. Though still embittered by not winning at least the silver medal, there was at least some satisfaction in what they had accomplished since coming together six months before.

Medal presentations and awards took place that Sunday evening. There was a lavish dinner for all teams in the tournament and, for Canada, a gathering later in the evening at the Canadian Embassy, where they were fêted with more of the same. The mood was good all round.

Next morning at 5 a.m., they boarded an Air Canada DC-8 for home.

FINAL TEAM STANDINGS

TOP 4 TEAMS	W	L	T	PTS	GOALS*
Russia	6	0	1	13	55-7
Czechoslovakia	6	1	0	12	32-15
Canada	5	2	0	10	33-15
Sweden	3	3	1	7	26-17

INDIVIDUAL STATISTICS

	G	A	PTS
Aleksandrov, Russia	9	9	18
Almetov, Russia	5	8	13
Starshinov, Russia	11	1	12
Pryl, Czechoslovakia	6	5	11
Loktev, Russia	5	5	10
Yakushev, Russia	3	7	10
Huck, Canada	4	5	9
Faulkner, Canada	6	2	8
Bourbonnais, Canada	3	5	8
Nedomansky, Czech	5	2	7
L. Nilsson, Sweden	4	3	7
Koks, Czechoslovakia	3	4	7

* SHOWING GOALS FOR AND AGAINST

George contributed six goals for Canada, two of them winners. It was the team's best placing in the tournament since 1962. They had finished fourth three years in a row.

Nothing in George Faulkner's hockey future would surpass the experience of the World Championship in Yugoslavia. It seemed fitting that playing hockey at the international level should perhaps highlight a career as varied and lengthy as his. Being a part of the national hockey program for that one time, being asked to share the same excitement and display the same hockey skills as those young kids sitting beside him on the bench and in the dressing room, many of them future NHLers, was a lifetime moment. The game at home would never be the same.

In the next few years, what followed this venture would be a somewhat lengthy and disappointing sojourn in Corner Brook, a short-lived professional re-run in Florida with Jacksonville of the Eastern Hockey League, and his final playing years in St. John's, which, among other things, would give him the chance very few athletes get to experience – playing on the same team with his son, both of them now members of the St. John's Capitals.

The Herder Memorial Trophy championships and Allan Cup competitions would continue to come his way; the exciting scoring prowess he had displayed would not begin to diminish for the next while. Even as newer and younger challengers came along, he remained at the forefront of Newfoundland hockey, but it would not have the same ring as those moments with Canada's national team at the world tournament.

Not that he was entirely finished with Canada's national team. There would be another experience coming his way a year later in the international arena, an unexpected and lesser role, and one he would not have to don the pads for.

1967-71

PART FIVE

THE SEMI-FINALS
1967-1971

20

THE CLOSING CEEBEES' YEARS

THE 1965-66 VERSION OF THE CONCEPTION BAY CEEBEES
under their new temporary coach, Alex Faulkner, were having a rough year. Alex had broken his wrist in game five of the season, back in December, and would not play again until the playoffs in March, about the same time George was scheduled to arrive back from Europe. The team struggled to hold a playoff spot in the five-team league, just barely ahead of the St. John's entry.

Alex's return coincided almost to the day with the return of brother George from the World Championships in Yugoslavia, himself bearing the remnants of a slight but bothersome groin injury. As so often happened in the case of a returning Faulkner from some kind of layoff, it was as if he'd never left. As the 1966 playoffs began, the Ceebees rolled over a surprised Gander team in games one and two in Harbour Grace, but back in Gander for game three, they were handily dismissed. The team suffered its worse loss ever: 15-7. It looked like "a game of fives": Dougie Squires and Jacques Allard of the Gander Flyers had five goals each, Alex Faulkner had five assists, and George had two goals and three assists.

The Ceebees would go on to outlast the Flyers in that series, but would miss the Herder this year, losing to the Corner Brook Royals, four games to one. The Royals had finished in first place, and their win over the Ceebees marked their third Herder Trophy, tying Conception Bay's record for the same period. Only the Buchans Miners in 1963 had managed to interrupt the victorious stretch by these two perennial winners. Just as the St. John's Capitals would go on to dominate the 1970s, it was the Ceebees and the Royals who held the reins in the 1960s, and as the 1966-67 season began, neither was quite finished just yet. Both great teams had one more Herder to go before the end of the decade. In 1967, it would fall to the Ceebees, in what many claim would be their finest year ever. Certainly, the drive for the Herder this year would end, for George Faulkner, in a flourish.

They called him "the Cobra." Twenty-two-year-old goaltender Gary Simmons, from Charlottetown, PEI, and property of the Detroit Red Wings at the time, joined the Conception Bay Ceebees for the 1966-67 season. It was a timely signing for George Faulkner. Brothers Alex and Jack had left once again for assignments in the professional ranks, this time both headed the San Diego Gulls. Meanwhile, George's sidekick on defence, Harold Stanley, had moved on to play in Grand Falls. This left a considerable gap in the Ceebees offensive and defensive game. Another addition that year was strongman and scoring ace Bern Fitzpatrick, a journeyman originally from Bell Island, but able to appear anywhere it seemed where a team needed strength and scoring power. Veterans Gerry Lahey, Jimmy Dawe and Jim Penney were expected to continue among the league leaders in scoring. Not far behind in this powerful scoring mix was George himself, contributing two-goal efforts throughout the season, and continuing his stalwart role as part on the team's defence. But it would be largely the play of Gary Simmons that took the team to a second-place finish, behind Gander, then on to the Ceebees' fourth Herder Memorial Trophy, and a first-time shot at Allan Cup* play. Local sports coverage that year describes Simmons as constantly "outstanding," often handling 40 to 50 shots per game. Few teams survive that kind of nightly barrage, let alone come away as winners as often as they did.

Games one and two of the 1967 Herder finals were played in Harbour Grace. After a close overtime loss in game one, with both goaltenders – Lyle Carter of Gander and Simmons – putting in brilliant performances, the Flyers came undone in game two, losing badly, 8-3. Game three, a crucial one for the Flyers in their own rink, went badly as well – another 8-3 bashing by the Ceebees.

----

* The Allan Cup is symbolic of seniority in amateur hockey in Canada. The 1967 Conception Bay Ceebees were the first Newfoundland team ever to play in this tournament.

After game three, with Gary Simmons again unbeatable most of the time, frustrating the Flyers' shooters all night long (while George is putting another four-point night in the record books), it looked as if the series might be all over. Game four was scheduled for Tuesday, March 21. That same Tuesday morning George received a long distance phone call, and heard a familiar voice on the other end saying, "Hello, Georgie ..." It was Father David Bauer, calling on a hunch from Vienna, site of that year's World Hockey Championships. Bauer always called him "Georgie."

"Georgie," Bauer continued, "we're over here in Vienna, and we're doing all right so far, but the guys are not having any fun. Why don't you pick up that guitar of yours and come over and join us? The team is playing okay but needs to unwind before the big game on Friday."

He was told his ticket would be at the Gander airport, whenever he was ready and if he could make it. The only problem was that he still had to play the fourth game of the Herder finals that night against Gander. If the Ceebees won, he'd have lots of time to make it to Vienna. If they lost, who knows?

The Ceebees lost Tuesday night's game, 3-1, though Gary Simmons gave another brilliant performance, handling 51 shots. The series now stood at three games to one, with the next day, Wednesday, a day off, and game five scheduled for Thursday.

Air Canada's timetable had the Newfoundland transatlantic flight scheduled to leave from Gander at 10:30 Thursday evening. George had contacted the airline earlier in the day and told them of his plans for a hasty exit after the game to make it to the terminal for the flight – if his Ceebees could beat the Flyers, and, if the game did not go into overtime. The game's starting time was, as usual, eight o'clock. "We'll do our best to accommodate you" was all they could tell him.

The game was a thriller from the start, and stayed that way until the final whistle, with the Ceebees finally winning by 5-4. It was the team's fourth and last Herder Memorial Championship. While the traditional on-ice celebrations and picture-taking were underway, George hurried to the dressing room, as planned, for the last-minute rush to make the flight to Europe.* A quick shower, he thought, followed by a change of fresh clothes, and he was on his way.

----

* The Ceebees' team picture that year shows George wearing civilian clothes, readying himself to make it to Gander International Airport on time.

"In those days the Gander dressing rooms had one big overhead bulb. I'd say a 500-watt bulb, in the centre of the room – that's how it was lit. I rushed in and Frank Moores came in behind me and he had a bottle of champagne with him. He popped the cork and where do you think that cork went? Here we are, in the dark, glass everywhere, and I'm thinking of nothing else but missing that airplane."

When things got back to normal and the room was cleaned and Frank Moores had left, George was finally underway once again. At the last minute he figured he'd celebrate by taking along a single bottle of Dominion Pale Ale with him on the plane. "I wasn't much of a beer drinker, but I wanted something to celebrate with, and that's all that was there." At the airport he learned that they had held up the plane some twenty minutes waiting for him. He rushed on board, beer in hand, and as he was being greeted by the steward and still trying to explain the delay, he was told "they would do better than that." They promptly seated him, replaced the beer with a glass of cold champagne, and then saluted their local hockey hero officially, as the plane began to taxi and make ready for takeoff.*

His return to Canada just a few days later marked the beginning of another first in the career of George Faulkner. This time he would lead the first contingent from Newfoundland to play for the Allan Cup. The Moncton Hawks proved to be too powerful for the Ceebees, who fell three games to one in the five-game series. However, there was nothing despondent in the team's reaction to the loss that year, nor in the minds of its fans back home. More than anything else, it showed the improved competitiveness of the Newfoundland game, led by the ever-exciting Ceebees, a competitiveness that would pay off years later, in 1986, for a team from Corner Brook.

---

* Despite the sonorous tones of both voice and guitar, George could not overturn another third-place finish for Canada in 1967. The protest against refereeing the year before did not have any effect on player interest – all of last year's players returned to compete for Canada.

21

THE CORNER BROOK CRISIS

AT THE END OF THE 1967-68 SEASON, GEORGE FAULKNER'S
tenth with the Ceebees, there was no sign of any kind of change happening to the
Conception Bay legends, and no indications from George that this might be his
last. The team had finished a turbulent season in typically strong fashion, in what
had become an exciting five-team race for the playoffs. As the decade drew to a
close, the league was becoming more and more competitive, and, with the exception of the lowly Gander Flyers, it was anybody's guess what teams might finally make the 1968 playoffs, and what would happen afterwards.

The final outcome showed only five points separating the first-place team
from the fifth in the standings. The Ceebees had managed only a fourth-place
finish behind the Grand Falls Cataracts, Buchans Miners and Corner Brook
Royals. At the end, the St. John's Capitals were an unbelievable two points shy
of making the fourth spot. The playoffs looked to be murderous.

After the Conception Bay Ceebees took the first two games at home against the
Buchans Miners, the playoffs had all the appearances of being just another "run
for the roses." The average hockey fan was beginning to feel he had been
down this road before, and knew full well what the ending looked like. Back
home for the next game in Buchans, the Miners, facing the impossible, probably
felt the same way. The prospect of winning four of the next five against Faulkner's
Ceebees looked intimidating enough, but to do so against the league's best
goalie, Gary Simmons, whose goaltending feats were becoming legendary, was
too much to ask. No one had ever won four straight against the Conception Bay
Ceebees.

But that's just what the 1968 Buchans Miners did. Outscoring the Ceebees 31-19, they took the series four games to two to move into the finals. It was an unimaginable feat, and perhaps the finest moment ever in the history of that great team. Sadly, they could not carry the momentum to the end, losing the finals that year four games to one to the Corner Brook Royals. The series wasn't nearly as exciting as the semi-finals had been, but, for the Royals, it nevertheless represented their fourth win on the Herder since their first in 1962. The win tied them with Conception Bay in total Herder championships. Ironically, the only team to break the grip held by these two teams during the 1960s was the 1963 Buchans Miners. The rest of the decade, up to now, had belonged to the Ceebees and the Royals.

The devastating loss to Buchans that year seemed almost ominous considering what was to occur before the start of the next NAHA season. It became a story that carried headlines for weeks in the local media, and apparently one that began to critically shake the league's foundations like nothing before. And it had all to do with a rumor, first whispered in October, that George Faulkner might be leaving Harbour Grace and the Conception Bay Ceebees. It seemed unbelievable that that the loss of one 36-year-old player could jeopardize the future of an entire organization, subsequently affecting the favourite pastime of tens of thousands of hockey fans. For the people of Conception Bay, the loss could only be compared to a death in the family.

The already heightened atmosphere surrounding the rumour was soon intensified by an additional rumour: the fact that he might be leaving to join the powerhouse Corner Brook Royals. The NAHA executive was suddenly looking at a volcanic blowup in its organization, with outcries and protests coming from all quarters, and little time to go before the scheduled season opener.

The truth was that George had been considering a business deal with the Corner Brook organization three years before, one which would have included the ownership of a small sports shop in the city. The arrangement, which never got off the ground, was being discussed with Ray Pollett, then president of the Corner Brook Hockey Association. "Had that deal been agreed to, I would have been gone three years before," George recalls. "The deal fell through at the time, and I simply returned to Harbour Grace."

Sports columnist Bernie Bennett of the *Evening Telegram*, broke the story in a big way in early October and followed the spin-offs and possible league casualties for a full two-week period. Emergency meetings at all levels were held. Headlines proclaiming "NO FAULKNER, NO CEEBEES" and commentaries on what might become of the NAHA season appeared as lead stories for days. "If the Ceebees are out, it's the beginning of the end," said one spokesman for the NAHA at the time.*

The prospect of starting the season with just five teams, three of which were "stacked," left Association President Terry Trainor of St. John's, perhaps the most vocal of all spokesmen, in the worst situation of all. Ironically, his St. John's Capitals, representing the biggest hockey centre in the province, would be most vulnerable to collapse should Faulkner decide to leave. Support from the city's business community was almost nonexistent, and without that teams survived on gate receipts only. "We can't compete with other centres. We can't get any backing from anyone." The loss of revenue from home games involving the popular George Faulkner and his Ceebees, Trainor maintained, would place his team in a "very serious situation."

Trainor's situation seemed paradoxical. While other centres were crying out for more local talent and thereby avoiding the expense and circumstances of using "imports," he was sitting in "the catbird seat," with the highest number of talented local players to pick from. For some reason, he could not make it work.

Similarly, the town of Gander, under President Eric Dawe, was feeling the same pinch and for the same reason: "The Ceebees have always been a big drawing card here ... We budgeted for this season having the Ceebees in ... We are going to have to make adjustments somewhere." Meanwhile, the body still in the operating room, the other centres added to the confusion by already getting together and seriously considering carving up what might be left of the Ceebees for their own gain.

It was beginning to look like the future of George Faulkner in Newfoundland hockey was, in fact, the future of Newfoundland hockey itself.

The deal was announced as final on October 11: George Faulkner would become the new manager of Humber Gardens in Corner Brook, and would join the Corner Brook Royals as the team's newest acquisition. In addition to his contract as stadium manager, George would receive an additional bonus from the

* *St. John's Evening Telegram*, October 16, 1968.

Royals, simply as "player." The three-year contract was a good one – a three thousand dollar salary increase – and George, as much as he hated the thought of leaving the Ceebees, was more than confident he had made the right move for himself and his family. He was soon to turn 35 years old. Few people knew that he had been overlooked every year, since first signing in 1958, for any kind of a raise, any kind of financial recognition for the successes the team had had, for the kinds of money and influence the Ceebees hockey team had acquired throughout the local hockey world. He had led the team to every pinnacle of senior hockey, both in Newfoundland and in Canada, with every kind of recognition coming his way except a financial one.*

It was totally unexpected that, only a few hours after he and his family had actually left for Corner Brook and stopped for an overnight visit with his folks in Bishop's Falls along the way, someone in the Ceebees organization finally woke up to the reality of what they were losing.

"I got a call from Lloyd Archibald of the Harbour Grace organization asking me – almost like he was in some kind of dream world – if I had signed anything "yet" with Corner Brook. I told Lloyd I hadn't, but I had given them my word, and I wasn't going back on my word, and that's where the matter ended. These guys had years and years to make me an offer, a simple raise of some kind, or maybe a small business proposition, and never did, so I was gone."

NAHA President Don Johnson, ever the level-headed overseer in many local hockey wars, summed it up this way: "You can't blame George. He has a wife and family to look after and it's a natural thing to do." This was a generous way of looking at the situation, given the league's new state of affairs. George Faulkner's Ceebees had been the league's biggest drawing card. There was also the crucial matter of time – whether the Harbour Grace organization could put together anything resembling a team with just a short time in which to do it. Meanwhile, Terry Trainor, the spokesman for St. John's, was still out there trying to find a "fairy godmother" to save his St. John's Capitals. Suddenly, one of the

---

* In fairness to the people involved in the Harbour Grace fish industry at the time, it should be noted that a new British fish company, Birds Eye, had taken over the Harbour Grace operation. It goes without saying that their interest in local sports matters would not be the same. At the same time, Frank Moores had moved on to Ottawa, leaving behind any further significant connection to George and the Ceebees.

strongest amateur hockey organizations in Canada faced the ugly prospect of going under. The water was already rolling on the deck.

In the meantime, George Faulkner knew that for him the worst was still to come: having to play against the team he had created and loved, and having to do it very soon in front of all those Conception Bay fans who had come to love him. Deep down, he wondered if he could do it. Despite the irritating money issues, the decision had been bittersweet, and for the first time in his life, he realized hockey was no longer just a game.

For Midge Faulkner, the move would mean a welcome and more personal change. Her hometown of Howley was relatively close to Corner Brook, making visiting opportunities with family more frequent. It was a great chance for her father, George Vardy, to spend time with them in Corner Brook, maybe even spend the entire winter with them while he took in as many games at Humber Gardens as he wished – most of the time having the best seat in the house.

The NAHA survived the 1968-69 hockey season, as did the Conception Bay Ceebees, but it was not a pretty picture for either. The loss of the league's top player was felt immediately in Harbour Grace. Despite having retained a lineup which included their spectacular goaltender, Gary Simmons, and regulars Gerry Lahey and Jim Penney, the sudden change of mind of Jimmy Dawe,* and the addition of Dick Power from Bell Island, the team could muster no more than eight wins in the forty-game schedule, a crushing last-place finish for the once-proud Conception Bay champions.

For the Corner Brook Royals, the season wasn't much better. They finished in fifth place, just ahead of the Ceebees, and missed the playoffs as well. George Faulkner's contribution in goals for the season was just six. It seems the two shining lights of Newfoundland hockey, almost in tandem, were becoming murky at best, after a decade of dominance and success. In fact, this would be the final year for the Conception Bay Ceebees. The organization was left to die and there would be no further attempts in the years to come to resurrect it. George Faulkner's "baby" would soon be history.

---

* Dawe had announced earlier that he would be leaving the Ceebees and returning home to play for Grand Falls for the 1968-69 season, then suddenly changed his mind and came back to Harbour Grace instead. Some say he was the first of the "paid" players to play for Conception Bay and that many others followed before the start of that season.

More than two-thirds of the way into the season, with just eight games or so remaining, the powers that be in Corner Brook hockey decided to remove its biggest name from the coaching ranks and demote him to the role of "just another player." Frank Dorrington was asked to step down as coach – in favour of George Faulkner. The confusion and sheer ignominy placed in Dorrington's lap defies description, but he stayed on as a player, nevertheless.

The move came as a desperate attempt to make the playoffs that year. The team was floundering badly, with only a few games remaining. Even George himself felt the awkwardness of the situation, but between them the two NAHA superstars put their feelings aside and continued the season, taking the team to another year in the playoffs. "I did it reluctantly. I was uncomfortable with the whole thing – the way it was done and all." He remembers in his first practice with them that he took them right back to the basics of the game of hockey, calling them to centre ice and asking the same questions he had asked the Ceebees years before: "'Do you know what we're doing here? Do you know the four fundamentals of the game?' And there was no one who could answer, not even Dorrington. Make no wonder we were in trouble."

The final insult in all this mess came when George stepped on the ice for the first game in Harbour Grace against his old team. Everyone in the rink seemed to jump to their feet at the same moment and began a chorus of boos that seemed to last forever. Only the "dog" in him could get him through this moment. He endured it as one tries to endure pain in front of a child, but the wound went deep and it was a moment he would never forget. The good times were really over in Conception Bay.

They managed to make the playoffs that year but lost in the semi-finals to the St. John's Capitals. If truth be told, the Royals were more than glad when it was all over, and glad that they had seen the last – at least for awhile – of their new and fearsome driving force – George Faulkner. As they cleared out their lockers at the end of that disappointing year, no one knew at the time – not even George himself – that it would indeed be the last time they would see him, at least in Corner Brook, and wearing the same team uniform.

In 1970-71, as he prepared to begin the third year of his three-year contract in Corner Brook, the Royals would have another surprise in store for the team and for its once-tenacious hockey star: they would break his contract, arbitrarily removing payment for his on-ice role as a member of the Corner Brook Royals, and now its new coach. They wanted him to play for nothing. The newly elected Corner Brook Hockey Association, under a new chairman, Joe Chaulk, decided they would cut Faulkner's income and only pay his salary as stadium manager. No more hockey bonuses. Yet, they expected him to continue to coach and play for the Royals as usual, and were more than surprised when told he would not. In effect, George made plans to sit out the entire year, although offers were coming in to play with other teams – for pay – a situation untenable under the existing residency rules. The matter ended there, and for the first time George Faulkner faced the prospect of a year without hockey, but under the circumstances he was determined to do so. Meanwhile, the new coach of the team that year would once again be "Danky" Dorrington.

A crisis for the league surrounding his move to Corner Brook now became a personal one. There were no options except to "sit it out" for the year while looking ahead to his next move. It would certainly have nothing to do with Corner Brook or the Corner Brook Royals.

In early autumn of the following year, 1971, as his contract neared its end and with few real prospects, one of the Royals' brightest young players (and a favourite of George's), a 20-year-old, strapping left-winger named Ernie Hynes, received a call, seemingly out of the blue, from someone associated with Jacksonville of the Eastern Professional League, asking if he would be interested in coming to play for them during the upcoming season. A new team was being formed in the city and they needed help wherever they could get it. As a further enticement to young Ernie, the team would pay all expenses, including travel, and hotel accommodations during the tryout period. And, they continued, did he happen to know of any other good hockey players "up there in New-foundland" who might be interested in joining the club? The same arrangement would apply to them, Ernie was told.

"Ernie didn't want to go down there by himself, and I guess he figured, where I wasn't doing anything, why not ask me along?" George actually had to convince the young man to take the opportunity to play hockey in the south. What could go wrong? There was the offer of a healthy salary, good accommodations and all expenses paid to come back if it didn't work out. "I said, 'Ernie, what have we got to lose?'"

Once the deal was struck with a team called the Jacksonville Rockets, Faulkner and Hynes were on their way. He would be back on the ice, playing hockey again, and this time not just anywhere. He was about to play, *and be paid for playing*, in the Florida sun.

The two left for Florida in October on a venture that would last only three months. Ernie Hynes had no sooner arrived, played maybe an exhibition game or two, before breaking his ankle and being placed on the team's disabled list. He wanted to come home right away, but the team, more impressed than ever with his potential, wanted to pay him to stay until he recovered. George was somewhat surprised he wanted out so soon: "I came home one night, maybe nine or ten o'clock after a game or a practice, and Ernie was packing his suitcase. I said, 'Ernie, where are you going?' 'I'm going home,' he said. 'I've got enough of this.'" And that was that. A case of homesickness more than anything else.

It turned out that the Jacksonville Rockets would fold soon after and drop out of the league altogether: a matter of poor attendance and a general lack of interest throughout the league itself. The Florida dream was quickly dissolving, but there were still no regrets. As they had figured from the beginning, they had had nothing to lose.

Before leaving for home, George received an offer to play for a team in New Jersey, under similar circumstances and salary as had existed in Florida. It was tempting, especially as he would at least have money coming in until the end of the year. But he was beginning to feel that it was not really the life he wanted anymore for his family. He decided to call Midge back home just to talk, to see how she felt about the New Jersey prospects, and he got a very clear-cut answer: "It's time to come home," she told him.

It was nearing December and they still had to make yet another move in time for Christmas – this time to St. John's – where, as things turned out, they would settle down for good. Hockey would still be an important part of his life but, in the future, more a recreation than a profession. In the meantime, other plans and interests would begin to emerge to finally give them a financial stability and family security that looked as if it would last.

1975 79

PART SIX

THE FINALS

1975-1979

22

"OLD SOLDIERS NEVER DIE..."

CHRISTMAS, 1971. ABOUT TO FACE THEIR FIRST ST. JOHN'S winter of sleet, fog, rain, and possibly snow, the Faulkner family settled in their temporary living quarters at Hillview Terrace while the search for a new home began. The feeling all round was that this is finally it – this is where they will settle, and the feeling was a good one. Plans were soon underway for a new lifestyle, both for George and Midge. After 13 years as wife, mother and homemaker, Midge decided it was time to return to nursing and registered with the local association to undertake a three-week refresher course before taking up full-time work in the profession. By chance, George came across an advertisement looking for people interested in real estate sales, and immediately began his own course of study with ABH Real Estate Ltd., ready to take on a new career as a licensed, full-time agent. The boys, Robert and Peter, settled in their new schools nearby, and were more than ready to settle into regular routines at home and in school. The family disappointments experienced in the last days in Corner Brook, and the unsettling short-term venture in Jacksonville, were now behind them. For the time being, life in the Faulkner family would be a practical affair: being together and making a living from anything other than hockey. The best hockey years were indeed over. The nomadic lifestyle, finally gone.

George knew his love for hockey would never diminish, and while he wanted to compete at the level he was used to, he soon learned it would never be the same. Brother Alex managed to talk him into joining the St. John's Caps until the end of the 1972 season, first as player, then as playing-coach, but injuries once again intervened for both, and they could do no more than sit by and watch as their team suffered through another forgettable losing season.

The following season, 1972-73, he was persuaded once again to continue to play at the NAHA level, this time through the enticements of brother Jack, now playing-coach of the Gander Flyers. "All I did was visit Jack in Gander in October for a moose hunting trip, and all of a sudden I'm wearing a Gander Flyers uniform." The Flyers had trouble getting enough players to ice a team that year, and the league decided to allow George, against normal league residency rules, to sign up with the Flyers for this one season only. It turned out to be another losing season against a now-dominating team from St. John's.

Apart from the losses he endured on ice, George was doing well in his new habitat in St. John's, as was his wife Midge, now well established on her own in nursing. They had soon bought a new home in St. John's, close to old family friends, and hockey was becoming secondary in both their social and professional lives. But it seems every small temptation to get back to the game was still irresistible. Midge knew what he was feeling each time and, as she had done all their married lives, gave him loose rein. "It was really just a pastime then, something to keep me occupied and out of trouble. Or maybe just out of her way. But I still loved the connection to the game, even though I was through as a player."

The St. John's Capitals, finally coming of age, were rolling into their third consecutive winning season and third Herder Championship in 1975 when the name George Faulkner suddenly appeared on their roster yet again, both as player and coach. It seemed there was just no way to let George Faulkner off the hook.* He still had that toughness as coach, could still handle the team's conditioning at every whim, while holding the respect of this new crop of players who hardly knew who he was. He was 41 years old and still whipping them into shape,

---

* George had appeared sparingly in the two previous seasons with the Capitals – winning the Herder in both years.

skating with them, hustling their routines as hard as ever, and showing them all what they never quite had as yet – the professional touch.

"There was a special moment for me that year and it was quite accidental. The so-called Caps "A-Team," many of the team's best players, were on an exhibition hockey weekend in Labrador when they ran into an airlines strike and couldn't get back in time for the opening playoff game against Corner Brook." It was left to Don Johnson, now a fill-in behind the bench for the stranded Capitals' coach, Bob Badcock, to scramble together whatever players he could to fulfill the NAHA commitment to the team's regular playoff dates.

One of those new faces Don signed up to play happened to be George's son, Bob, fresh out of university ranks and showing pretty good stuff as a player himself. "There wasn't too much to it. We took a couple of shifts together – me on defence and Bob up front – and managed to keep the Royals off the score sheet each time. But I don't know who was more scared or awkward-looking though, me or Bob." What George didn't know, until it happened, was that the cagey Don Johnson saw a moment in local hockey history coming together in that game and had the two Faulkners, father and son, do a couple of shifts together on defence – just for the record. Bob remembers it all vividly: "I hit the ice half scared out of my mind and thinking: 'the minute I get the puck I'm handing it off to the old man. I don't care what happens.'"

The Faulkners held the fort in that circumstance as well, managing a sweet two-game victory over the surprised visitors from Corner Brook, and getting their names on the score sheet several times. The stranded "A-Team," meanwhile, made it back from Labrador in time to continue the series and move on to another Herder Trophy Championship.

At this stage, you would think an occasion such as playing in a senior hockey final (and winning) with your 18-year-old son alongside would be highlight enough to say, "That's it. It can't get any better than that." But for the ever-restive George Faulkner there would be one more moment, one more year before he would finally reach that point, and simply admit that it was time to go.

Which brings us almost to the end of the story.

The 1979 NAHA season had two entries from St. John's joining the league: a team called the "Blue Caps" and a collection of young players who would be known as "Mike's Shamrocks," brought together by an affable St. John's businessman, Mike Squires. Squires was almost as devoted to the game as

George himself, and his great ambition was finally realized: he had his own hockey club. His Shamrocks managed to acquire the services of a well-known and well-liked former St. John's player, Jimmy Byrne, as head coach, but in his wisdom Mike Squires wanted someone of George Faulkner's calibre to help – in this case to take on the role of assistant coach (defensive).

George, and perhaps to a lesser degree Midge, was delighted with the offer. He was back in business.

Twenty years before, in the 1958-59 season, he had come close to winning his first Herder, and standing behind the bench in 1979 among "Mike's Shamrocks," he couldn't help thinking how this would be a great way to finish it up: one more Herder. Midge agreed, but made it clear that either way, this time he had reached the end.

The Shamrocks, in an acclaimed team strategy that focused on "defensive" hockey, swept past their fellow Blue Caps, 3-1, in a five-game semi-final, and continued on to win the Herder from brother Jack's Gander Flyers in a seventh-game, "sudden death" encounter. Mike Squires had his first Herder Memorial Trophy, and George Faulkner, his ninth and last.

Eleven forty-five on a Sunday morning in February 2011 finds 77-year-old George Faulkner suiting up in dressing room #3 at the Mile One Centre in St. John's, preparing for the first of two recreation games this week. He still wears #17, on a jersey remarkably similar to the original New York Rangers sweaters he and his brothers wore in boyhood. Skates tied and comfortable, he reaches for a hockey stick – the envy of everyone else in the room – a gift from a young Newfoundland NHL star, Ryane Clowe, made of titanium and worth $250. A far cry from the birch pieces his father carved for him years ago for his games on the Exploits.

His teammates and opponents are a makeshift bunch of 30-, 40-, 50-, maybe 60-year-olds scattered about the same room. The buzz of enthusiasm in the room before they get started is almost tangible. For George, on this occasion, the shifts on defence will no longer be of 50- or 60-minutes duration – those days are fifty years gone.

Fifty years.

Go back another ten years and you have him on his way to Quebec for a tryout in the professional ranks. He was 17 then and, as far as anyone can tell, he had been skating for 13 years before that, most of it on his beloved Exploits River.

This is what makes his story so complicated. There seems to be no beginning and no end to his place in the game of hockey. Another difficulty in telling his story is in tracking the overwhelming collection of tributes, rewards, and honours that have come his way.

Eventually, such recognition found its way into academia – an Honorary Doctorate from Memorial University of Newfoundland, delivered by way of an oration that, quite appropriately, takes George back to the time of Moses. The analogy being that, like Moses, he never did make it to the promised land of the NHL, but instead drifted in the land of the Moab – i.e., another, maybe lesser, world of hockey.

His story is unique. His family's story equally so. Five boys born in a Newfoundland wilderness, destined to play hockey at a level unknown anywhere in the land. A father, Lester Faulkner, either through his own innate love of the game, or with some special kind of prescience or other, somehow knowing what lay ahead for his boys: preparing them, day and night, year after year, to play the game.

And then, living to see it all come true. Three of them would be the first in Newfoundland to become professional hockey players: George, Alex and Jack.

Of course, it was the time: the uniqueness of that river place at that time in Newfoundland history, that echoed what was happening in neighbouring Canada, on all those other outdoor rinks and rivers across a frozen land.

However, there would be no real Moses here, no wilderness into which any of Lester's boys would be set adrift. Instead, they would always manage to find just a sheet of ice, sitting anywhere, where they could play.

162

APPENDIX I

1. CHAMPIONSHIPS:

A. QUEBEC LEAGUES

1951-52	JUNIOR "B" – QUEBEC JUNIOR HOCKEY LEAGUE
1953-54	JUNIOR "A" – QUEBEC JUNIOR HOCKEY LEAGUE
1954-55	LEAGUE CHAMPIONSHIP – QUEBEC HOCKEY LEAGUE
1955-56	LEAGUE CHAMPIONSHIP – QUEBEC HOCKEY LEAGUE
1955-56	CANADIAN CHAMPIONSHIP – (EDINBURGH TROPHY)
1957-58	LEAGUE CHAMPIONSHIP – QUEBEC HOCKEY LEAGUE

B. NEWFOUNDLAND HERDER MEMORIAL TROPHY

1952-53	GRAND FALLS ALL-STARS
1959-60	CONCEPTION BAY CEEBEES
1960- 61	CONCEPTION BAY CEEBEES
1964-65	CONCEPTION BAY CEEBEES
1966-67	CONCEPTION BAY CEEBEES
1972-73	ST. JOHN'S CAPITALS
1973-74	ST. JOHN'S CAPITALS
1974-75	ST. JOHN'S CAPITALS
1978-79	MIKE'S SHAMROCKS

C. INTERNATIONAL WORLD ICE HOCKEY

1966	TEAM CANADA: BRONZE MEDAL WINNERS

2. AWARDS AND ACHIEVEMENTS:

A. First Newfoundlander to sign professional hockey contract
B. Voted 'Best Newfoundland Hockey Player'
C. Voted Newfoundland's 'Athlete of the Century'
D. Newfoundland Sports Hall of Fame
E. Manitoba Hockey Hall of Fame
F. Doctor of Laws, honoris causa, MUN, 2010.
G. Torch Bearer – 2010 Vancouver Winter Olympics
H. Torch Bearer – 1992 Newfoundland Summer Games

APPENDIX II

HERDER MEMORIAL TROPHY
1958-1968

WINNERS AND RUNNERS-UP

1958-59	Grand Falls	(Conception Bay)
1959-60	Conception Bay	(Grand Falls)
1960-61	Conception Bay	(Gander)
1961-62	Corner Brook	(Conception Bay)
1962-63	Buchans	(Corner Brook)
1963-64	Corner Brook	(Buchans)
1964-65	Conception Bay	(Corner Brook)
1965-66	Corner Brook	(Conception Bay)
1966-67	Conception Bay	(Gander)
1967-68	Corner Brook	(Buchans)
1968-69	Gander	(Buchans)

GEORGE FAULKNER: PERSONAL STATISTICS

YEAR	GAMES PLAYED	GOALS	ASSISTS	POINTS
1949-54	None Available			

SHAWINIGAN FALLS CATARACTS

YEAR	GAMES PLAYED	GOALS	ASSISTS	POINTS
1954-55	59	18	25	43
1955-56	52	17	16	33
1956-57	55	19	26	45
1957-58	51	19	17	36

CONCEPTION BAY CEEBEES

YEAR	GAMES PLAYED	GOALS	ASSISTS	POINTS
1958-59	14	20	13	33
1959-60	13	11	11	22
1960-61	10	10	16	26
1961-62	7	3	6	9
1962-63	16	12	14	26
1963-64	20	15	24	39
1964-65	20	19	45	63
1966-67	40	35	46	81
1967-68	40	34	35	69

CANADA'S NATIONAL TEAM

YEAR	GAMES PLAYED	GOALS	ASSISTS	POINTS
1965-66	22	11	13	24

NAHA COMPETITION

YEAR	GAMES PLAYED	GOALS	ASSISTS	POINTS
1968-69	36	6	31	37
1969-70	32	14	37	51
1971-72	26	12	23	35
1972-73	33	13	27	40
1973-74	2	0	1	1
1974-75	16	2	11	13
TOTALS	283	162	293	455

Source: *Newfoundland and Labrador Senior Hockey – A Trip Down Memory Lane,* Jerry "Stats" Elliot, 2010.

APPENDIX IV

SHAWINIGAN FALLS CATARACTS:
STATISTICS FOR "THE THREE MUSKETEERS"

1954-55

	GAMES PLAYED	GOALS	ASSISTS	POINTS
Connie Broden	62	27	35	62
George Faulkner	59	18	25	43
Eddie Kachur	59	25	14	39

1955-56

	GAMES PLAYED	GOALS	ASSISTS	POINTS
Eddie Kachur	64	31	34	65
Connie Broden	61	17	40	57
George Faulkner	52	17	16	33

1956-57

	GAMES PLAYED	GOALS	ASSISTS	POINTS
Connie Broden	68	20	29	49
George Faulkner	55	19	26	45
Eddie Kachur	32	12	12	24

1957-58

	GAMES PLAYED	GOALS	ASSISTS	POINTS
George Faulkner	51	19	17	36

TOTALS

	GAMES PLAYED	GOALS	ASSISTS	POINTS
Connie Broden	191	64	104	168
Eddie Kachur	155	68	60	128
George Faulkner	217	73	84	157

APPENDIX V

WHERE THE PLAYERS COME FROM

1957-58 NHL STATISTICS

Of the 105 players registered in the NHL this year, the following is a breakdown of the numbers coming from different regions of Canada:

Ontario – 53
Quebec – 24
Western Canada – 26
Maritimes – 2 (Nova Scotia: Parker McDonald, PEI: Forbes Kennedy)

From an article published in the *Montreal Gazette*, February 11, 1958.

**CANADIAN NATIONAL TEAM
1966 WORLD ICE HOCKEY CHAMPIONSHIPS
LJUBLJANA, YUGOSLAVIA**

TEAM MEMBERS

Manager	Father David Bauer (Kitchener, Ontario)
Head Coach	Jackie McLeod (Swift Current, Saskatchewan)
Goal	Seth Martin (Rossland, British Columbia)
	Ken Broderick (Toronto, Ontario)
	Wayne Stephenson (Fort William, Ontario)
Defence	Terry O'Malley, Captain (Toronto, Ontario)
	Gary Begg (Winnipeg, Manitoba)
	Barry MacKenzie (Toronto, Ontario)
	Lorne Davis (Regina, Saskatchewan)
	Harvey Schmidt (Regina, Saskatchewan)
Forwards	Roger Bourbonnais (Riviere Qui Barre, Alberta)
	Paul Conlin (Granton, Ontario)
	Ray Cadieux (Ottawa, Ontario)
	Fran Huck (Regina, Saskatchewan)
	Morris Mott (Creelman, Saskatchewan)
	Jackie McLeod (Swift Current, Saskatchewan)
	Marshall Johnson (Birch Hills, Saskatchewan)
	George Faulkner (Harbour Grace, Newfoundland)
	Billy MacMillan (Charlottetown, Prince Edward Island)

APPENDIX VII

QUEBEC ALL-STARS, MARITIME TOUR
APRIL 1957

OPPOSING NEWFOUNDLAND TEAMS

CORNER BROOK

Gerald Dwyer, Gordie Staples, Rod Kennedy, Doug Hillis, "Monk" Colbourne, Bob Colbourne, George Aucoin, Mel McQueen, Austin Taylor, Charlie Harris, Jake Critch, Roger Colbourne, Cyril Vardy, Pat Power, Ed Roche.

GRAND FALLS

Clobie Collins, "Bucky" Hannaford, "Sham" McInnis, Mun Pond, Harvey Howse, Terry Jesseau, Al Folkes, George Howse, Cec Thomas, Neil Knight, Heber Rideout, Vic Grignon, Jimmy Temple, Ralph Cook, Wats Goobie, "Blondie" Bartlett.

BELL ISLAND

Joe Penney, Bill Northcott, Bill Power, George Connors, Cyril Power, Hubert Power, Neil Kennedy, Pat O'Brien, Hal Sheppard, Gord Taylor, Gordon Skanes, Don Skanes, Joe Byrne, Martin Craig, Kevin Craig.

ST. JOHN'S

Irv Walsh, Bob Evans, Len Coughlan, John Fitzgerald, Tom Stone, Lloyd Cooke, Carl Browne, "Fa" Murphy, Cy Hoskins, Jackie Withers, Lloyd Roberts, Jack Ryan, Ray Bowe, Charlie Walsh, Maurice Colbert.

NEWFOUNDLAND ALL-STARS

BELL ISLAND	Bill Power, George Connors, Gordie Butler.
BUCHANS	Hugh Wadden, Phil Bowes, John Murphy.
GRAND FALLS	Clobie Collins, Alex Faulkner, "Sham" McInnis, "Bucky" Hannaford, Don Clarke.
ST. JOHN'S	Lloyd Cooke, Len Coughlan, Jackie Withers, Irv Walsh.

APPENDIX VIII

The following is taken from a conversation with Doug Moores, a lifelong friend of George Faulkner. Moores practices law in Bay Roberts, Conception Bay, and was one of the first graduates of the Harbour Grace minor hockey system. Hockey has been an integral part of his life ever since, both as player and organizer. From those early beginnings in Harbour Grace in 1958, he has played the game at all levels, beginning in the early 1960s with the MUN Varsity squad.

THE GOLDEN AGE OF HOCKEY

I was ten years old when George Faulkner arrived in Harbour Grace. We had just opened a new arena, and just as quickly, it seemed, we had a professional hockey coach as well. His job was to build a hockey program in the community and, more importantly to many residents, to build an NAHA team. It was Frank Moores who started it all. Frank wanted a hockey team, and he would go to any lengths to get one. He was a great sportsman himself, always on the go with one thing or another. He loved the Ceebees like no other. Maybe as much as I did.

George took on the full recreational program for Harbour Grace, and I guess I spent as much time around him playing soccer and softball in those early years as I did later on, with hockey. I only lived a gunshot down the street from him and became a close friend right from the start. I was a goalie, sometimes a privileged one since I had access to professional coaching from someone who had played the game with the best in the country.

The Ceebees' years, with the three Faulkners in their prime and dominating the league the way they did, were pretty exciting times for everyone, especially for the people in Conception Bay. But it wasn't always just about winning. It was the excitement of watching such skilful players, seeing the speed and finesse of their skating and passing.

The stadium was filled for every game, year after, win or lose, and we didn't always win. People came to the games in droves, by train and road, to see our Ceebees. I know of many instances where, if the team was playing in Grand Falls or Gander, fans from Twillingate would cross Notre Dame Bay to Lewisporte and then hitch a ride to the game that night. They came to see the best players in the history of our game, and, at the time, among the best in Canada: Lahey, Stanley, Dwyer, Dawe, Simmons, the Penneys, Kelly, Martin, Hunt, Coady and myself. George always put the local guys first, always wanting to give them a game, and a job, if needed.

As for George Faulkner and his brothers, they were exceptional people: disciplined, dedicated on and off the ice. I think George's biggest quality, both as a person and an athlete, was leadership. People wanted to play for him, and, if they could, to play with the Faulkners. I watched his "conditioning" program over and over: how at the end of an hour or an hour and a half of a hard practice (probably the second for the day), he would finish by having the team skate the figure eight, following his lead, for 45 minutes. And no one would ever catch him.

Everyone talks of all those games where he played the full 60 minutes, night after night. I remember having a conversation once with a fellow when George's name came up. The guy obviously knew George pretty well. "George Faulkner?" he said. "What a player! He spent more time at the ice than Abe Kean!"

The Faulkners had so much ability. Alex had it all from the blueline in – quick, raw talent. Natural ability. He was a one-dimensional guy with an eye for scoring – a quickness with the stick that no one else had. Jack, on the other hand, came to the game late and was groomed by George as more of an all-round player. He was terribly strong, with a tremendous shot and was a heavy shooter with lots of natural ability, always right up there with the leading goal scorers. Put three of them together and every game – no matter what the score – was worth the price.

Let me finish by saying that, apart from hockey, George Faulkner was a charming, unassuming person – a gentleman. I never heard him say anything stronger than "Gee whiz" when things didn't go right. He had a pleasant personality, always there to help and encourage his players, never critical of them in public. He was the best in so many ways. Certainly, he was the best who ever played the game in Newfoundland.

When you think back on it, the game that was played back then – in the 1960s Ceebees' era – will never be seen again. It was the best. The golden age of hockey.

BIBLIOGRAPHY

BOOKS

Abbott, Bill. *Herder Memorial Trophy*. St. John's: Breakwater, 2000.

Blake, Jason. *Canadian Hockey Literature*. Toronto: University of Toronto Press, 2010.

Cole, Stephen. *The Last Hurrah*. Toronto: Viking, 1995.

Elliott, Jerry. *Newfoundland and Labrador Senior Hockey – A Trip Down Memory Lane*. St. John's: Print Three, 2010.

Irvin, Dick. *The Habs*. Toronto: McClelland & Stewart, 1991.

Quarrington, Paul, Ed. *Original Six*. Toronto: Reed Books Canada, 1996.

Ronberg, Gary. *The Violent Game*. Englewood Cliffs, N.J. : Rutledge Books, 1975.

NEWSPAPERS

Western Star

Advertiser

Montreal Gazette

Quebec Chronicle-Telegraph

The Daily News

Evening Telegram

ACKNOWLEDGEMENTS

I'VE HAD MANY FRIENDS who've endured my humble literary attempts in the last few years, notably my children – Lynn, Lori, Michael and Lucille. I think the fact that I was writing family stories at the time might have helped them get through it. Similarly, a group of friends have read and commented on my attempts (and paid me little mercy when they did). They took more delight in content than literary merit, and the result was always entertaining for me and for them: Ed and Mary Noonan (always keen to read and help), Kevin Breen (my biggest fan) and Tom Burke, a fearsome critic of many things literary.

A renewed acquaintance with an old college roommate from years ago proved helpful and very encouraging in reviewing early drafts of the book. Thank you, Larry DeBlois. Two very important sources who came into play half-way through the work – Jerry 'Stats' Elliott of St. John's and Wayne Hollett of Burin. Your work proved immensely valuable and time-saving in laying so much important information at my fingertips. Many thanks.

The Pretty family played a part as well: Greg, Ann and Mary. The most they'd read belonging to me before this began was the family diary at our country place. Nothing like family.

To my dear and sometimes unwilling personal editor, Sharon, who was to ascend to the more significant role of indexer at the end, a big thank you. You saved me many hours of tedious labour and kept up the encouragement throughout.

To Alex and Jack Faulkner for their insights and encouragement in bringing so many aspects of the story to the forefront. Hearing their stories first was very special. I hope I did them justice.

To the very professional people at Breakwater: Annamarie Beckel, Rhonda Molloy, Erika Steeves, Kerry O'Neill and Rebecca Rose, a sincere thank you. To Paul Bowdring of Editors & Co. for your dedication and hard work as the project neared completion, my thanks.

Lastly, to the one who got me into all this – Lillian Moakler – a close and life-long friend of the Faulkners, particularly Midge. The two worked together in the nursing profession for many years. About a year ago, Lill suggested I talk to George about undertaking the project. Lill, I hope it was worth it.

TOM ROSSITER is a retired educator, teacher, administrator and curriculum co-ordinator. He has co-edited high school texts in English literature for the provinces of NL, NB, ON and PEI, including a teacher resource manual for use in the teaching of poetry in high school. He has edited several anthologies of children's writings. Several of his short stories have appeared in local media over the past 10 years. *Faulkner: A Hockey History* is his first attempt at a major writing project.

TO MY WIFE, MIDGE, A LOVING FRIEND AND COMPANION.
Thank you for the unwavering love and support over the many years. I will always love and miss you.

– George

www.ingramcontent.com/pod-product-compliance
Lightning Source LLC
Chambersburg PA
CBHW080503110426
42742CB00017B/2984

* 9 7 8 1 5 5 0 8 1 3 7 6 0 *